SHATTERED DREAMS AT RAINBOW'S END

A Novel about Inheritance and Infidelity

CHRISTOPHER HORNE, PHD

outskirts
press

DEDICATION

To my dear friend Bert: your never-failing understanding and encouragement and your steadfast brotherly love and counseling helped sharpen my mind.

To my wife, who carried the dream to this day—the dream Donald held, and Mary passed on to you. There are no words adequate to thank you for who you are and whose you are. By your love, you helped strengthen my soul.

To my children, whose patience and compassion never stopped in times of sorrow and who, by your actions, kept the dream alive.

Godspeed, all

TABLE OF CONTENTS

ACKNOWLEDGMENTS

Thanks to Dr. Ben, Dr. William, and Dr. Eric.

The author and editor thank Cheryl C. Cohen, Director of Membership Investment at the Orange County [NY] Chamber of Commerce for her editorial assistance.

FOREWORD

Except for its Epilogue, which is nonfiction, this is a novel, one based on the events in a family Dr. Christopher K. Horne knows well.

Because it is a novel, the reader is alerted that the dialogues are approximations, as are most other elements "quoted" in the book, and the actions and rationales of the characters are as interpreted/created by the novelist, rather than being so closely rooted in reality as to be testimony.

As a novel, it falls in the category of "a cautionary tale," with two major themes: how inherited property can become not a blessing but a burden, and how hard it is to maintain one's marriage vows. These challenges produced the "shattered dreams" of the title.

Christopher Horne wrote this within half a year, dutifully sending me (his coach and editor) his additions weekly and accepting my proposed changes (generally quite minor) with good grace. He was eager to convey the lessons this family learned about bequests, adherence to a moral code, and marriage. In doing so, he has depicted some characters who struggled with temptation, with more or less success, and some who showed nobility of soul in the face of great disappointments.

We hope the readers of *Shattered Dreams* will be both entertained and edified.

Douglas Winslow Cooper, Ph.D.
WriteYourBookWithMe.com
Walden, NY
Spring 2018

PREFACE

"Dreams"
by Langston Hughes

Hold fast to dreams.
For if dreams die,
Life is a broken-winged bird
That cannot fly.

Hold fast to dreams.
For when dreams go,
Life is a barren field
Frozen with snow.

"Picking up the pieces of a shattered dream is better than
having no pieces to pick up at all."
— Matshona Dhliwayo

"The dreams and passions stored within hearts are
powerful keys which can unlock a wealth of potential"
— John C. Maxwell

"You are never too old to set another goal
or to dream a new dream."
— C.S. Lewis [Extract by CS Lewis
© copyright CS Lewis Pte Ltd.]

I wrote this book to honor a forgotten World War II hero who dreamed of family values: honor, loyalty, integrity, and love. His dream was shattered by difficult life choices made by his wife and family, resulting in tragedy and triumph. I have tried to include some hard lessons learned in the process.

So often, others have said or written what we wish we had the skill to state. Still, we must have the courage to try, and this is what I have done. We live and learn!

Christopher K. Horne, Ph.D.
High Point, NC
ChrisHorne111@gmail.com
www.christopherhorne.com
Spring 2018

PROLOGUE

3 July 1988

"I cant drive, fifty-five!" Charles sang at the top of his lungs with the radio blasting. And he wasn't. The speedometer on his Mustang read seventy as the lush green grass and tall North Carolina pine trees rushed by.

With Raleigh and another college semester behind him, Charles was headed home to Greensboro and the next step in his plan to become wealthy and famous. He was looking forward to the trip, having recently completed final exams as a sophmore engineering student.

Well, he thought, "I may not become rich and famous, but at least I will get my college degree." Well, maybe not either of those things, but a job with Dad repairing and renovating rental properties would give this poor engineering student some much needed cash.

"Hello there, do you need life insurance?" the radio announcer yelled out.

"No, I don't! I need a life." Being where Charles was in life was akin to sitting at a stop light waiting for it to turn green. Only this stop light had two more years of intense study and exams before it would change. And even there would be a master's degree, an MBA and a PhD after that.

When he arrived around 10:30 that morning, his mom, a housewife turned elementary school assistant teacher, was not home, but his dad's 1984 pickup truck was backed in his garage. Charles could see lumber and tools hanging out the rear.

Dad had just bought the little truck after 15-plus years of using an old Buick to carry his carpentry tools around town. Perhaps his neighbors thought he was poor, with a downtrodden vehicle, but modesty was part of his character...and so was kindness. The truck made carrying stepladders and 2x4s much more practical than using a loaded-down family car.

"Dad, where are you?" Charles shouted in the one-story house which stood among the tall trees, a large vegetable garden and the old wooden shed. "Where are you?" would be a phrase the young man would ask himself over and over into his middle years.

Oddly enough, Charles could not find Dad in the garage nor in the house. Then, as he walked back outside through the screen porch, above the rustling of tree leaves, he could hear someone whistling in the back near the shed.

The shed was in the back yard tucked among the tall pine trees where Dad stored lumber and other equipment and most importantly where he would dream. Memorably, it was where Mom was stung by a swarm from a hornet's nest-the only time Charles saw Mom take off her clothes outside the house and run for the water hose to rid herself of the little monsters. While running half naked, Mary screamed, "Get me the water hose!"

Dad was content, at 63 years of age, now retired as a property manager; he was a former postal letter carrier and a World War II hero.

"Dad, I always wanted to ask you where all those holes and marks on your face and chest came from?" Charles asked his father. "Those are from D-Day, The Battle of the Bulge and The Hurtgen Forest in France and Germany."

Charles was always in awe of this man who bore 13 shrapnel wounds—some of which were still markedly visible on his body during the summer, when they worked shirtless on his rental houses.

Dad did not like talking about World War II, but the pictures he had brought home of the piles of dead bodies at concentration camps—mounds of dead Jews, young and old, male and female, all emaciated—made a massive impact on Charles's view of the world and impressed on him what Dad and his generation stood for. He was deservedly proud to be free, free to pursue his dreams.

Dad was very fond of Charles, his youngest, the last child of three offspring and, according to Mom, his "pride and joy." His father encouraged him to attend college rather than be a house painter or construction worker.

Charles also worked for his older brother at his auto body shop in the summers, but the relationship they had was shallow and perfunctory, unlike the one Charles had with my father, whose deep, abiding love was part of his dream.

"Help me with these boards - they are a little heavy", Dad instructed Charles. The boards were oak, strong, hard and would be used to construct a new front porch. Charles would paint the front porch battleship gray, Dad's favorite color on his rental properties.

Dad had spent all that morning procuring lumber, nails, and other tools they would transport in the little white truck to their new 80-year-old mountain farm house situated by the New River in Ashe County, NC.

Dad, Donald by name, never thought of the "cabin" as being his, but as his family's, to enjoy the scenery and "good times."

"This weekend will be some hard work but all of the family can enjoy it", Dad said with a modest soft voice to Charles.

Within 15 minutes of Charles' arrival, he could see Dad with sweat pouring down his face, shouting, "Let's go to the mountains!" Your mother will join us tomorrow."

Charles knew "tomorrow in the mountains" would be the completion of a new front porch, his loving mother and girlfriend Abigail would join them for fried chicken, green beans, trout fishing and the relaxing mountain air.

Dad was a friendly man, yet one with both backbone and morals. Despite being 40 percent disabled due to wounds suffered as a foot soldier, aggravated by his long hours as a mail carrier and property manager, he remained steadfast in his pursuit of his goals and dreams.

As a property manager, he had witnessed the destructive racial gunfire in a 1979 shoot-out between the Black Panthers and the Ku Klux Klan. He had found dead bodies in Section 8 government housing, a grim reminder of the deaths he saw firsthand in Europe. These gruesome sights, so different from his "doodling" with pencil as a child and drafting with a T-square and compass as a Pittsburgh art student, provided more motivation to pursue his dream.

The old mountain house was so remote in the North Carolina mountains, the natives used horses to reach the parcel of land situated along Big Horse Creek. Dad's truck would make the 1/4 mile path along the creek to a two-story framed house originally built around 1910.

After arriving at the old mountain house, Dad said "Charles, let's get to work on this porch; I'll pick up some creek rocks."

Charles got to work quickly on the front porch. It had been failing for several years. The farmhouse once fed and kept warm (by a wood stove) the Miller family, who used the 40 acres to make a living raising dairy cows, tobacco and seven children.

Upstairs, meat hung in one room, next to the elder room. Downstairs, the floors were coming apart, as was the foundation, originally built with large flat rocks from the creek 100 feet away. Dad and Charles were picking up these large rocks and carrying them by hand to the front porch they were rebuilding.

Dad used old hand tools: a hand saw, "20-penny" nails, and a large hammer. Dad's drawing prowess, learned after the war, and carpentry skills, passed on from his forefathers, enabled him to repair the porch with ease. He taught Charles how to use a T-square to "square our work" and how to use a carpenter's level to lay the horizontal 2x6s for the new porch foundations.

Dad and Charles got started at 11 AM, the mountain air would be a blessing for the hot summer afternoon. Charles could see Dad struggling to move the large, heavy rocks from the creek to the porch.

The 63-year-old war vet called Donald looked more like a 73-year-old by today's standards. Nevertheless, Dad was anxious to get the porch repaired. He looked forward to tomorrow, when his work was done, he would be seeing his wife of 39 years. Dad did not talk much but Charles knew he was pursuing his dream.

Although not obese, Dad was considered overweight for his age but his physical disability from the War did not deter him from carpentry work. After an hour of working on the cabin's front porch, Dad was quiet, sweating profusely and appeared unusually tired.

He stopped and said, "Let us go see Bob."

Bob and Dad were war buddies. Bob was also a World War II veteran, not in the European theatre, but he had fought in the jungles of Burma.

As a young college kid in the presence of a war-torn jungle rat, Charles endured a tough time being teased about his apparently innocent "book smarts," which were much less important to Bob than "street smarts." Charles was always taught to respect his elders. Despite his frustration with Bob's dirty mouth, Charles went along and said little.

Dad and Charles took the little white truck up the 2000-foot mountain road to see Bob that crisp spring day. They together drove up the narrow mountain road to Bob's screened-in porch for a brief chat.

Dad and Charles pulled up the nearby mountain ridge to Bob's cabin in the little white truck. The short and stocky Bob with a gray beard was splitting wood with his axe.

"Hey Don, whose this college kid you have with you?".

Dad and Bob cut up a bit, retreated inside Bob's small cabin then Dad paid him $100 in cash for some tools. As they sat on the porch with the beautiful mountain scenery in front of them, Charles noticed Dad's complexion changing from his natural reddish color to white and pale. With a weaker voice Dad said, "We better get going Bob - we have a front porch to fix."

They started back down the mountain. Dad appeared anxious to get back to his porch work. As he was driving, about a third of the way down the hill, his head slumped forward, and he grabbed his chest with his right hand, leaving the steering wheel briefly uncontrolled. Charles was scared. This dusty gravel mountain road was so narrow that the drop off to a much lower elevation was only three feet away on the side.

Charles knew something serious was wrong with Dad. All plans for "today" and "tomorrow with Mom" changed in a moment. The foot soldier who had taken gunfire for his platoon and compatriots and had received over a dozen shrapnel wounds was now literally fighting the steering wheel—and the steep mountain—for his life.

As his left hand extended toward his father, Charles wanted to comfort his body, but he knew his hand needed to grab the steering wheel of the pickup truck. They, together, managed to steer the truck the remaining quarter-mile to the bottom of the mountain, where Rainbow's End Lane intersected the paved state road.

By this time, Dad's head slumped all the way over, his body limp, and in a low, strained voice, he whispered, "Son, you will need to drive. I cannot make it by myself.... I cannot steer any longer."

Charles pulled his nearly lifeless, 185-pound body across his stomach and switched places with the dreamer, who was now suffering a massive heart attack.

The nearest doctor was about six miles away, but arriving at the small country office, Charles found it was closed for the day, so he drove rapidly, heading toward the nearest hospital along hilly, winding roads that kept his speed at about 40 mph. Despite appearing lifeless for 45 minutes in the passenger seat, Donald then recovered: his pain subsided at the hospital, and he even managed to walk into the Emergency Room of Jefferson Hospital.

At that point, Charles knew in his heart his dad's dream still existed. They had hope.

Myocardial infarction, commonly known as a heart attack, occurs when blood flow decreases or stops to a part of the heart, causing damage to the heart muscle. The most common symptom is chest pain or discomfort which may travel into the shoulder, arm, back, neck, or jaw. The extreme chest pain Dad had experienced was due to a massive heart attack.

Dad stayed in the hospital for about an hour to get checked out, but the doctor on duty said he had a massive heart attack and needed Coumadin. At the time, Charles understood the drug to be a "blood thinner." Coumadin is an anticoagulant medication to help prevent clots from forming in the blood. In mountain slang the doctor told Charles, "Your father had a massive heart attack. He will need intensive care we cannot offer at this small hospital." In private the doctor told Charles the Coumadin was not adminsistered soon enough. In his heart Charles was devastated that he did not get his father to the hosital soon enough and a stroke was imminent.

Dad was transferred by helicopter to West Forsyth Hospital. Charles followed the helicopter flying overhead in their little truck, going east, until the aerial vehicle was nowhere in sight. Surprisingly, he arrived at Forsyth Hospital before the helicopter; the scene was much like what you see in movies: the copter landed, and the body was rushed to the emergency room.

The emergency room tests lasted briefly until Dad was admitted to intensive care.

Mom had been preparing for this day to be a joyful time in the mountains, a beautiful day; it now appeared like a shattered dream, and her world was turned upside down. As her husband Donald was rolled into the emergency room from the helicopter, she ran to meet him and found the World War II hero with his thumb up saying,"We'll get back to the mountain cabin soon."

Over the next month while Mom comforted Dad in ICU she kept thinking sbout the mountain farm and her many loyal friends including Boyd and Billie and Bob who would offer encouragement and reassurance and hope.

They knew the end was coming. One day, with many tubes in his body and not being able to talk, Dad lifted his hand and gave a "thumbs up," then he fell asleep for good. After a month in the ICU, Dad's conditioned worsened to where his body was in a vegetative state.

On July 2 late in the evening, Mom left the ICU to get some long-awaited sleep while Charles's brother stayed in the ICU room.

Dad died July 3rd, 1988, but his dream lived on ... in Charles, at least.

CHAPTER 1

DEATH OF A PATRIARCH

In many ways, Donald Spencer was a dreamer.

Growing up in the Great Depression, on a dirt road in a small mill town in central North Carolina, Donald, even at 7 years old, "doodled" on a notepad, drawing figures of cartoon characters and nature.

His mother and father, textile mill workers, worked at a factory, operating knitting machines that made socks. Their life was not the stuff of dreams.

THE CRASH OF 1929

The heady days following the end of the "Great War," World War I, lasted about a decade. Too soon, the stock market crash of 1929 left his family eating rations of beans and taters grown in their backyard garden behind their small, four-room frame house. Life was hard for his parents, trying to "make ends meet," but young Donald would eventually live the "American Dream" ... well, not quite and not immediately: his dream was to be stifled by World War II, followed by physical ailments, marital strife, greed, and corruption.

The 1929 stock market crash had made many in the nation ration their food, leaving Donald and his family hungry from time to time, but the crash would contribute in the early 1980s to his passion for investing, along with real estate wealth-building. Like many in what has sometimes been called "the Greatest Generation," an early retirement enabled him to fulfill his dream; in his case, it was moving to a secluded mountain cabin with his wife, Mary, along with three children and five grandchildren, and then sharing the 100-year-old farm with many friends and members of his extended family.

Donald's younger sister, Dorothy, called her brother "Buddy," an affectionate nickname from their childhood together playing jacks and hop-scotch in the backyard.

WORLD WAR II

Fifteen years later, Buddy served as Dorothy's confidant when they exchanged letters during his boot camp days at Fort Hood, Texas, before taking a long ship ride to England in preparation for the dreaded Normandy invasion.

The World War II draft made kids like Donald Spencer into real men, fast.

Donald had graduated from high school in 1942, but his plans to work in the textile mill and start a construction business were cut short. On 7 December 1942, "the Day of Infamy," six months before he graduated, over 2000 U.S. troops were killed by the Japanese air attack at Pearl Harbor. Simultaneously, Adolf Hitler's German Army marched into the Baltic states and declared war on the United States.

In 1943, a spry and friendly nineteen-year-old Donald left North Carolina to join thousands of other young men at Fort Hood, Texas, to be a part of the U.S. Army's 4th Infantry Division. The division participated in battlefield maneuvers in Florida, starting in September. After his fall training exercise, they arrived at Camp Jackson, near Columbia, South Carolina, on 1 December 1943.

At Camp Jackson, his division was alerted by the Allied Commander Dwight D. Eisenhower to prepare for overseas movement; they were then staged at Camp Kilmer, New Jersey, beginning 4 January 1944, prior to departing the New York port on 18 January 1944. The 4th Infantry Division sailed to England, arriving on 26 January 1944.

Donald moved up the ranks from private in the Army, rapidly promoted to sergeant in the 4th Infantry Division that assaulted the northern coast of German-held France during the Normandy landings, landing at Utah Beach, June 6, 1944.

In one account, a commanding officer is said to have exclaimed, "If you survive your first day, I'll promote you." The officer had promised this to the men in the boats crossing the English Channel preparing to storm the hedgerows of Normandy, a promise dramatically fulfilled for 20-year-old Donald.

On June 6, the landing crafts' doors opened some 100 yards from the French beachhead. Despite enemy fire and nausea from sea sickness, Donald waded in the chest-high ocean surf, fortunately escaping serious injury. He was a member of the 8th Infantry Regiment of the 4th Infantry Division, the first surface-borne Allied unit to hit the beaches at Normandy on D-Day.

From July 1944 to the closing days of the war—from the first penetration of the Siegfried Line to the Nazis' last desperate charge in the Battle of the Bulge—Donald served as a foot soldier.

He fought in the thickest of the military action, helping take the small towns of northern France and Belgium, enduring frostbitten feet in foxholes, the brutal winter in the Hurtgen Forest and the near-death combat which earned him the Purple Heart in the Battle of the Bulge. Eventually, he accumulated 13 wounds, and had shrapnel embedded even in his steel-plated *Bible* in his shirt pocket.

Donald Spencer earned the Purple Heart and was awarded two Bronze Stars for Bravery and Valor.

Donald would later recount the war with much emotion: his encounters after surpassing the beachhead, the surge into France where the dead from both sides lay twisted, mangled, and torn, some half-buried in overturned earth, livestock with their stiff legs thrust skyward in death lying everywhere, along with burned vehicles and an occasional stray cat roaming the scorched earth.

When Donald's squad was ordered to move out on the attack, his body was taut with fear. The Sherman tanks took the lead, while Donald and the infantry advanced and began to feel stronger. His commanding officer ordered the men to shoot up everything in sight. Since no Americans were ahead of Donald's outfit, his orders were to shoot and shoot. Many of the Germans they encountered were not shooting, so the young Donald was hesitant to shoot them. Donald told the teenager Charles, "I've never been able to erase the thought of killing them from my mind."

ART SCHOOL

After returning from the war, the "doodler" attended the Pittsburgh School of Art, perfecting his drawing skills. The contrast between school and war could hardly have been greater. Like most World War II vets, Donald was not quite sure what career path to take in the fall of 1944, so he left his small North Carolina home for the colder rugged steel town of Pittsburgh, Pennsylvania. His mother, Tillie, had grieved for her son in the prior two years while he faced cold, frostbite and gunfire; now she would say goodbye to her son again as he pursued his dream.

At the Pittsburgh School of Art, Donald not only perfected his cartoon figures, he also learned mechanical drawing, using lead pencils pressing on an oak board constructing lines, angles, and circles with a T-square and compass. The square would be used draw angles of ninety degrees, and the compass to construct arcs and circles.

These drawing techniques using the square and compass would be emblematic ways to "square his work." Along with using a level to lay horizontals, these instruments would aid him in constructing right angles and perpendiculars while building steps, porches and walls with hammer, hand saw, and nails on his rental properties in his future, the 1970s and 80s.

While Donald doodled at art school, producing Disney-like characters, he wrote letters at night from his one-room apartment to his mother, to his sister Dorothy and to a new girlfriend he met while off-duty, in College Station, Texas.

Lucile was a blue-eyed 19-year-old recent high school graduate, the daughter of an army lieutenant. Donald met her in nearby Waco, Texas. The newly enlisted privates of the army stationed at Fort Hood received leave for one weekend. On a Friday evening, Donald found himself at the Waco Diner, a pub-like place where the 20s singles met to mingle.

The Waco Diner was a local favorite for tasty food, friendly atmosphere, and good music. Private Donald, a modest young man, would visit the Waco Diner, eating hotdogs and drinking an RC Cola while listening to big band and jazz music over the radio, music by legends such as Glenn Miller, Ella Fitzgerald, and Benny Goodman.

Donald was a gentleman, having learned the "art of chivalry" from his father and mother. This helped him approach his new friend Lucile at the drink counter, the White counter, not the one for African-Americans, "Coloreds" in the language of the time.

Lucile was with her parents, making his introductory move even more challenging. Donald managed to introduce himself to Lucile's father. Donald walked over to the booth and approached the father first with a firm handshake while Lucile smiled. "Sir, I am Donald Spencer of Company B in The U.S. 8th Division, and I would like to meet your daughter", the young private proclaimed. Lucile smiled at Donald as he introduced himself, and his brazen smile did most of the work, but their encounter was brief. Lucile would not leave Donald's mind; he returned to the diner the next evening to find Lucile and her girlfriends enjoying the sounds of Ella Fitzgerald: "Blue skies smiling at me; nothing but blue skies do I see," lyrics Donald would resonate with as he would eventually ask Lucile for her telephone number as he left the diner for the last time. He was to return the short distance to Fort Hood and, soon, to the dreaded shores of Normandy. But on this night, part of his dream was crafted as he wrote Lucile from his cramped, one-room apartment in Pittsburgh, the art student, World War II hero, a searching 21-year-old future patriot.

Donald received a letter from his mother telling him that the U.S. Postal Service was hiring letter carriers; she begged Donald to come home. For Donald, the only letters he was interested in were ones from Lucile. Furthermore, the cold steel town resembled his home not at all. Home for Donald was where the heart lived, where Mom, after a long day at the mill, would prepare tasty warm meals—cornbread, pinto beans, turnip greens, and slices of ham, all of which tasted much better than the C-rations of crackers, sugar tablets and sausages he ate as a foot soldier in the cold, smoky air of France and Belgium.

LETTER CARRIER

Donald returned home in 1946, after his sabbatical at the Pittsburgh School of Art, and in 1947, after working short-term construction jobs in his home town, he gained employment as a letter carrier with the U.S. Postal Service. He carried letters to a section of town which had some 1,000 citizens, mostly the poorer population, laborers in the hosiery and textile mills and mechanics. He carried a 10-pound satchel on his shoulder, walking four to five miles each day.

Walking and pounding the gravel roads were routine for Donald, having journeyed by foot from the shores of

Normandy to Paris, some 75 miles. In contrast to his trip of death through Belgium, where bomb craters big enough to swallow a jeep were so close together in some areas it was difficult for the tank drivers to zigzag through, the letter carrier job was a piece of cake. Unfortunately, Donald's satchel weighed heavily on his wounds of World War II, especially the egg-size wound to one shoulder. But the modest, smiling, and friendly Donald would not let the shoulder pain stop his dream to meet his future wife.

Donald's hometown was like most small industrial settings in the 1940s, recovering from the Depression. Thousands of young American men had spent years away from their wives and girlfriends because of World War II. You can imagine the joy Donald experienced upon being reunited with his family, but he longed for a Lucile-like friend, a pal like the beauty he met in the Waco Diner, and did not get to know. This blue-eyed darling, later in life, wrote to him on her death bed.

Donald was determined to live his dream and would not wait for Lucile but rather spotted two cute, petite sisters home from school one day, sitting on their battleship-gray front porch waiting to receive the day's mail. Donald soon found out that one sister, Mary, was home to care for her young father whose health was deteriorating rapidly due to alcoholism. Mary's father was a short-term truck driver who was fired from several textile mills jobs due primarily to drunkenness on the job. It was his alcoholism that would fill Mary with contempt for that drug and one day hurt her so much that the emotional pain remained a family secret until her death in 2015.

Donald's curiosity for this brown-haired, brown-eyed stunner with a curvy figure would not diminish. When he went home after seven years of carrying the mail, his thoughts were on Mary, who lived literally and figuratively "across the railroad tracks" in a poorer part of town. Picture a little one-story wooden frame house with white clapboard siding, no air conditioning, and no indoor toilet. Chickens roamed the back yard, where nourishment for the young family was marginal with a lazy drunken father. In contrast, picture the two beautiful sisters, wearing sun dresses with their hair flowing in the breeze.

Mary's mother grew up on an old farm built right after the Civil War. By today's standards her mother had a third grade education. What the family lacked in formal book smarts was made up by hard labor. She was the oldest of thirteen children, poor by most standards even then. She worked as a seamstress in the hosiery mill she walked to every day.

When Donald did not have a letter to deliver to Mary's home, he still found a way to see her. His dream and his heart burned for a wife. He soon found out that young Mary attended church, was single and articulate—even eloquent—despite her impoverished setting and living conditions. Capturing Mary's attention would not come easy for Donald, even with her deep desire to be a mother and raise a family. Caring for her alcoholic dad was an emotional strain, aggravated by verbal abuse. Despite that abuse, she felt obligated to care for her father. While her sister smoked Winstons, Mary remained purer in thought, spirit, and behavior.

In many ways, the early postwar era was a socially conservative time. Gender roles for men and women were, more often than not, traditional and very clearly defined. When World War II ended, many women who had worked in factories during the war returned to home and the domestic way of life. Mary stayed home with her sister to care for her father and pursue quilting.

For two years, Donald carried mail to Mary's home. As Mary's father sobered up, she accepted Donald's invitation to go out on a date to the downtown movie theatre. In 1949, for recreation in small-town America, families window-shopped and went to the movies. Donald borrowed his father's '46 Buick; he had not yet saved up enough money to buy a used car.

On their first date night, Donald and Mary watched the movie *The Clock*, about a World War II soldier on a two-day leave in New York: Joe meets Alice; they end up falling in love with each other, and they decide to get married before Joe must return to military camp.

For Donald this was the perfect story to watch with Mary, a happy ending of sorts since he did not have to return to war. When the date was over that Friday night, Donald opened the door of his dad's 1946 Buick Roadmaster and walked Mary back to her front door. Like most modest, moral ladies of the 1940s, a kiss on the cheek was all Miss Mary would offer. But this was just right for Donald; his dream was coming true.

Not so very long after their first date, on a sizzling summer Sunday in 1949, Donald and Mary were to be wed in a Baptist church. Mary's wedding dress was a modest white gown with lace sleeves and a long veil—she made her own dress as an example of the self-reliance she exemplified as a Depression-era child. Her jewelry was minimal—a pearl necklace and matching earrings. Donald's mother bought him his suit, a three-piece navy-blue outfit and a blue tie.

The only "thing" missing this wedding day was the bride's father, gone missing the morning of the much-anticipated event. Mary's mother tolerated her husband's alcoholism and womanizing for many years. Mary's father was unable to support the whole family, so Mary's mother walked to the nearby textile mill and worked as a seamstress who made seventy-one dollars a week.

At the wedding, Mary's mother remained quiet until her alcoholic husband was not found at the church. In a panic, Mary recalled the years spent caring for her 51-year-old father, a poor boy of the Depression born on a South Carolina farm with nine brothers and sisters. Mary's Uncle Elmo retreated to find Mary's dad; he was in a drunken stupor at home. An expected joyful day for Mary turned out to be tearful instead; Mary cried during the one-hour delay in the wedding ceremony, a delay taken to allow the drunk to stumble his daughter down the aisle, the smell of alcohol following him.

Donald had waited and waited for this part of his dream to come true, and it had.

REAL ESTATE

After seven years, Donald left the Postal Service. The weight of the letter satchel inflicted too much pain on his war-torn shoulder, and his once-frostbitten toes could use some rest after standing and freezing in the foxholes of Europe and now walking the North Carolina roads delivering mail.

During the 1950s, racial tensions appeared calm compared to today. Nevertheless, a kind-hearted Donald and most of his white friends wanted little to do with black people. Even so, the South of the 1950s was the land of fire hoses aimed at black people who dared protest so-called "Jim Crow" segregation laws.

Donald was a man who wanted to give back to his community by serving in his church and civic organizations, but also as an entertainer. The Jaycees were a group of men dedicated to improving the community. Despite much good they did, they also supported a Broadway-like show that included "minstrel men." Donald was an "end man," blackfaced and carrying a tambourine. His jokes by today's moral standards were clean, but the Al-Jolson-like performances that made everyone either laugh or smile would be considered racially insulting today.

Blackface is a form of theatrical makeup used predominantly by non-black performers to represent a black person. The practice gained popularity during the 19th century and contributed to the spread of racial stereotypes such as the term "coon." Donald's wife, Mary, was mostly naive of the blackface insults and like most white people, just accepted the activity. Later in life, the theme of racial harmony would contribute to Donald's dream.

Donald met several powerful community leaders while

serving as a "Jaycee Jollie End Man." The leaders included Edward, who owned an affluent real estate firm. Donald's friendly character and his war-hero status caught the eye of Edward when he attended one of the Jaycee vaudeville shows. Edward soon offered Donald a job as a property manager, attending the affairs of government housing.

In the 1930s, the federal government began a program explicitly designed to increase and segregate America's housing. The government's efforts were primarily designed to provide housing to middle-class white families. African-Americans and other people of color were left out of the new suburban communities and pushed instead into urban housing projects.

Donald's goal to work in real estate came true. He became a property manager for a small residential firm, and he managed government-funded, "Section 8" housing in the part of town where he carried mail, where he met his second love, Mary. Donald became actively involved in managing many residential homes occupied by very poor black people.

As a property manager, Donald did not have to endure shoulder pain from the letters and satchel pulling on the wound he suffered in the Battle of the Bulge some ten years prior. The thirty-seven-year-old was ready to take on what he thought would be a desk job, but which turned out to be a lot of work outside of the office. His experience doodling on paper as a boy, braving German gunfire for his squad, and learning how to use a T-square to draw right angles would come in handy for this new prodigy of a real estate executive. Donald thought he would be managing the properties occupied by the white folk, but Edward needed someone who could take care of the housing no other employee wanted to manage.

Entering 1960, real estate markets were growing, kindled by the pent-up demand and the surging economy. A second Housing Act was passed in 1954, when President Eisenhower held office. This act was a notable change because it focused on rehabilitating the slum areas, including Donald's territory.

Then, later, the Housing Act of 1956 made amends for the first housing act by giving relocation payments to all who were displaced, including the poor black families Donald interacted with and collected rent from.

Before Donald became a property manager, public housing was discriminatory. Many of the previous federal programs were of no aid to minority groups and instead focused on white people—those not of the lowest economic status. In fact, through the 1950s very strict policies were in place in many housing facilities. Pregnant women who were not married could be evicted, and property damage was charged with outrageous fines.

Donald managed properties occupied by poor Black families, and race relations were progressive in his small town, but there still existed segregated facilities: black restrooms, black seats in restaurants.

In February 1960, black high school students for the all-black school across the railroad tracks where Donald managed Section 8 housing, walked into a nearby lunch counter. The store was set up so that blacks and whites could order food, but only whites could eat there. After a few minutes, the students sat at the empty seats and stood behind seats occupied by white patrons, who quickly left.

The sit-ins occurred regularly, and violence erupted near Donald's office; he witnessed with flashbacks WWII gunshot fire that had left both whites and blacks injured.

A day after the local newspaper editorial was published about the incident, the town Mayor created the Human Relations Committee to examine the issues behind the sit-ins. This interracial committee was considered the first of its kind. Donald had met the town mayor when Edward shared lunch with them a few weeks prior.

When the mayor asked Edward to serve on the committee, he recommended Donald instead. Donald's participation in the committee was enlightening to the kind-hearted man who dressed up in blackface on weekends in skits that made fun of blacks. Through the Committee and witnessing the gunfire at home, he would now gain an appreciation for the struggles of the African-American community.

The Human Relations Committee recommended a trial period of integration for all store lunch counters. However, the Committee had no enforcing power and the stores refused to integrate. Donald was frustrated that something simple like open seats for all people was not accepted by business owners.

In the late 1960s and into the 1970s, Donald grew as a man with community service and by befriending poor African-Americans who lived in the housing projects and company rental property. Many of them were uneducated, with little appreciation for clean housing practices or the maintenance necessary to prevent structural or facility problems. Donald's family was unaware of the countless number of poor tenants he helped in some way.

Meanwhile, Donald and his wife, Mary, raised their two children. The family was considered in the community as "all-American," since Donald could support his wife and two children without himself having a college education—they were living the American dream, Donald's dream.

The oldest child, Deborah, was a quiet girl with a few friends; she mostly kept to herself in the modest three-bedroom home near city center. It was 1963 and Deborah was entering her teen years. A teenager in the 1960s was surrounded by historic events, including the Vietnam War, MLK's death, JFK's death and more. Deborah and her friends began to develop a "hippie" or "flower child" point of view.

Meanwhile her little brother, Danny, was a tinkerer, played with toys, and built toy machines. Despite a compelling spirit, Danny was a mischievous child, getting into trouble several times with his mother and at school. Once Danny's mother gave him ten cents to buy ice cream at grade school. When Danny came home and still had the money, Mary questioned

Danny, who told her his poor behavior got him punished and prohibited him from buying the dessert.

In the 1960s, there were no cell phones or email or Facebook and most teenagers had daily chores—Donald's wife made sure the kids worked around the house. Both Deborah and Danny attended school, which was a simple environment. You read out of books with no hands-on work. Teachers had complete authority over students. A student who misbehaved might have gotten hit with a ruler.

In 1960, the family moved to a rural area only five miles from the city center. Donald had made profits from rental property and decided it was time to build a three-bedroom ranch home on two acres of land where he could grow crops and tinker in the yard, much as he did as a young boy.

In 1966, the third child was born, a boy they named Charles, the name given on Christmas Eve before a snowy Christmas day. Charles was not a quiet baby, keeping Mary awake most nights for almost three years.

By this time, Deborah was in high school, and the nightly crying baby was too much for her. She set her sights on graduating from high school and leaving town for college.

Mary's time was spent primarily with Charles, leaving Deborah and Danny jealous of the new lad. In fact, Charles was considered Donald's pride and joy and received extra school tutoring, piano lessons, and trips from East Coast to West Coast.

There may have been some favoritism toward Charles, but this is natural for the last child where the older siblings chose to either leave home or resent their younger brother. In fact, Danny was the youngest for twelve years under family conditions which had now abruptly changed, so it is no wonder he was jealous.

Meanwhile, Donald worked day and night to improve his rental properties, worth more than $350,000—not bad for 1970.

Donald had attended a small high school through the eleventh grade, but World War II resulted in his being drafted for D-Day. He never attended college, so he always had a dream for his children to advance their learning beyond high school.

Deborah attended Gardner Webb College to study liberal arts. This did not last long. In 1970, she became engaged to a psychology graduate, Johnny Jetson. Johnny was a preacher's son from South Carolina. Deborah and Johnny were married in 1971. Soon thereafter, Deborah became a mother, while Johnny attended Bible College.

Donald and Danny often did not see eye-to-eye, despite their similar skill sets in carpentry, mechanics, and construction projects. Donald had learned in World War II the fragile nature of life: that mortality was a German bullet away and not to be taken lightly; to fear God and treat others as you would want to be treated. Danny, on the other hand, was mischievous, stubborn, and argumentative, lacking in self-confidence, yet tireless in his personal pursuits even at the expense of relationships.

One day, Donald asked his son to clean his room, littered with machine parts and tools. So, Danny moved his tools and parts from his bedroom floor to the crawl space under the house, which was where Donald had stored his own working tools. The lack of respect for his father's space soon bothered Danny, but he did not have the courage to tell his father he was sorry. Despite Danny's determination to make something of himself through arduous work as his dad had done, this would not be the last time Donald would be disappointed in Danny for his self-centered behavior.

Charles was now twelve years old. Danny remained jealous of Charles. One evening, Danny told Charles that he would be skipping dinner to go work on his car at a friend's shop. Danny told Charles not to tell his mother where he was going. Mary was adamant that dinner was an important time for the family to come together each day.

When Mary arrived home from the grocery store, she asked where Danny was. Charles told her he skipped dinner to work on his car and hang out with friends. This lack of respect infuriated Mary, so she called the friend's house and asked Danny to come home. When Danny arrived home, he confronted little Charles and chased him out back, where the 25-year-old beat the 12-year-old Charles. Then, Danny made up to his mother by sweet-talking her and helping her install some framed portraits of the family. Donald was too busy to notice, engrossed in constructing drawings with his T-square and compass in his home office.

Charles grew as a teenager, playing sports and making decent grades. Danny stayed active with Charles in sports but did not attend church with Donald and Mary. Danny was too busy for family matters. Despite Danny's estrangement from family meals and deep conversations, Donald felt sorry for Danny and helped him secure a bank loan to purchase an old warehouse that Danny would convert to an automobile repair shop.

A few years earlier, in high school, Danny's poor grades had undermined his self-confidence in academic affairs, so he pursued building machines and working on cars instead. Danny's business matured from his 18-hour workdays, while his new wife, Martha, remained employed to provide health insurance for Danny and their new son.

Donald's rental income grew, and his dream appeared to him closer on the horizon. Mary decided to use her domestic skills caring for her children in the classroom and in 1984 was employed as a teaching assistant in an inner-city school in the same neighborhood as Donald's rental property among the poor white and black folks.

Charles spent Saturdays painting Donald's rental properties in low-income neighborhoods where drug deals occurred, and gunshots could be heard from time to time. Charles learned the carpentry skills his father had learned from his dad in the 1930s.

Donald was a leader in the community. His World War II battlefield experience and what he learned as property manager for government housing, as well as being a new grandfather to Deborah's new children, helped him to serve effectively at the Salvation Army.

Donald enjoyed being a grandfather. He and Mary would visit Deborah's new family. Meanwhile, Charles became jealous of his parents' involvement with Deborah's family.

Donald and Mary were active in the United Methodist Church, where Donald was a leader. Donald's special female friend was Polly, the pianist and musical leader of the Jaycee Jollies minstrel show. Polly would come and visit Donald, Mary, and Charles on Christmas Eve, and they would tell each other stories. It was the only occasion during which Mary allowed smoking in the house; Polly was a chain smoker with a deep laugh and a natural talent for musical instruments. Around this season, Charles extended his talent for performing magic tricks to Polly's high school Christmas show.

Charles was a quiet teen who spent most of this time playing baseball, wrestling, and excelling in the high school band. Notably, Charles and his mother took several long trips around the United States. While Charles performed magic shows and played sports, his father began to spend more and more time away from home, either working on his rental properties or volunteering for Big Brothers/Big Sisters, a youth organization that fosters relationships between fatherless kids and community leaders such as Donald.

Mary noticed her husband spending more time with Big Brother/Big Sisters than coming home to spend time with her and Charles. Even Danny noticed his father seemed more absent than usual, but Mary kept the home moving along with domestic duties, school teaching, and church activities.

Mary worked at the nearby elementary school. On her way home, she observed Donald's car at a rental property. As several weeks passed, she frequently saw Donald's car at the same rental property. After some investigation, Mary determined that the home was occupied by a 40-year-old woman, the mother of the fatherless boys Donald was mentoring.

Mary became upset. She suspected something was not right. She questioned Donald that evening. Most men would deny such an allegation of promiscuity, but Donald did not respond. So, the next day when Mary drove by this home where the woman lived, she knocked on the door and found Donald with her.

Mary came home and cried, then opened her *Bible* to a verse she read while caring for her alcoholic dad in her teens: "Dear friends, I urge you, as foreigners and exiles, to abstain from sinful desires, which wage war against your soul" (*1 Peter 2:11*). Poetry and the *Bible* would one day comfort Mary again in her pain.

That same day, while Charles was helping Danny at his automobile shop, Danny received a phone call from his mother, who was crying and informing him that Donald was caught at the home of the two boys he was mentoring, with their mother.

Mary and her children had never expected their father to be caught straying. Charles, 16 years old, was disappointed in his father. He naturally did not know what his response should be and so remained quiet. The family's disappointment and anger lasted only a few weeks. Mary and Donald decided to work out the dilemma, with Donald planning to retire in the next year to spend more time with his wife. The behavior necessary to mend the brokenness was forgiveness.

Forgiveness only requires one person. Despite the pain Mary felt from Donald's unfaithfulness, she chose to forgive him. The reconciliation began and a new, wonderful journey between the two commenced.

Forgiveness only requires one person, but marriage reconciliation requires two people. That week after the straying was caught by Mary, Charles recalled Mary and Donald talking in their bedroom and then heard them making love. Their happiness increased over the next few years, as Donald's dream stayed alive.

Charles graduated from high school in 1986, stayed in touch with a girlfriend, Abigail, and made a few friends at the university. Back home, Donald continued to build his rental properties while Danny continued to grow his auto repair shop business and become a community leader like his father.

Donald exchanged his salaried position as property manager with the real estate company for retirement, but he remained owner of more than 15 properties he had accumulated and invested in since the 1970s.

His property management employer gave him a Kennedy rocking chair as a retirement gift.

Upon receiving the rocking chair, Donald was asked by a colleague where he would sit in the chair, to which Donald replied, "Rocking chairs are for old folks who have little to do—I have the rest of my life to live."

Donald's dream had survived the Depression, World War II, a marriage crisis, fatherhood, and now the entering of a new chapter, retirement. But rest and relaxation were not for Donald anytime soon. His dream required work.

CHAPTER 2

RAINBOW'S END LANE

Donald retired in 1987 after 29 years with the same real estate firm. It was time for Donald to settle down in his last chapter of life, to spend his last years in the mountains. Deep down, Donald knew he was mortal, unlike his son Danny who thought himself to be invincible. Their sister, Deborah, had three children by this time. Charles was studying engineering at the state university.

Meanwhile, Donald and Mary continued to search for the ideal retirement locale. Ashe County, a corner of the Blue Ridge Mountains, offered a wide variety of activities for the perfect getaway.

Donald's dream was coming true in the planning stages of finding a retirement location. One of the fundamental moral principles Donald practiced was from the Ten Commandments: "Honor thy father and mother." He learned this from his boyhood days, helping his father work in small construction projects and doing chores for his mother.

Mary and Donald had discussed where they might retire in a second home. The beach was considered; they visited the North Carolina coast on a sizzling summer weekend, and then, the following week, cool mountain air overwhelmed the couple, and they decided to check out three properties in the

North Carolina county of Ashe. The country they grew to love was in the corner of the state, nestled near the intersection of Virginia and Tennessee where the native folk had settled in the 1800s.

After investigating and considering alternatives, Donald and Mary offered to buy a 40-acre farm for $28,000. The 1910 frame house snuggled at the base of a 2700-foot mountain along the Big Horse Creek, only three miles from the Virginia border and ten miles from Tennessee. It was time for Donald to settle down in his last chapter of life, to spend his last years in the mountains. His dream would not come alive without some sweat equity, some "elbow grease" and some pain.

The history of Ashe County prior to the 18th century is somewhat obscure. The Cherokee, Creek, and Shawnee Indians hunted, fished, and battled each other within the region. Peter Jefferson led a surveying party in 1749 to establish a line between North Carolina and Virginia, as early settlers and visitors alike were unsure as to which state they had settled in. In 1752, Bishop Augustus Spangenberg, head of the Moravian Church of America, made the first recorded visit, in search of 100,000 acres of land for settlement purposes.

References to hunting expeditions date back to the 1770s, David Helton's being one of the earliest, Daniel Boone's certainly being the most famous. Ashe County's first recorded deed is dated 1773. The settlers who came to the mountains were primarily of English, Scotch-Irish, and German descent. They came to buy, settle, and farm the cheap, fertile bottomlands and hillsides in the region. Some migrated from the North Carolina Piedmont and the Coastal Plain. They came by foot, wagon, or horseback, entering the area through passages such as Swannanoa, Hickory Nut, Gillespie, and Deep Gaps.

Though he was looking forward to retirement, Donald was in pain, and Donald knew pain well, having suffered multiple gunshot wounds in the Hurtgen Forest during the winter of 1944.

The Battle in the Hurtgen Forest was one of the bloodiest battles in World War II, the longest single battle ever fought by U.S. forces. The trench warfare character of this battle made it known as "the Verdun of WWII." The Battle of Hurtgen Forest was a series of fierce clashes fought from 19 September to 16 December 1944 between American and German forces on the Western Front in the Hurtgen Forest area, about 50 square miles, just east of the Belgian-German border. The Hurtgen Forest battles cost the U.S. First Army at least 33,000 killed or wounded, including both combat and non-combat losses; German casualties were 28,000.

Donald received two Purple Hearts—one awarded for his bravery in the Hurtgen Forest and one for bravery in the Battle of the Bulge.

For the Hurtgen Forest award, Donald's Purple Heart medal inscription reads "bravery while wounded in action," quite fitting for Donald's dream and appropriate for a World War II hero.

In retirement, Donald's pain was enhanced by his frustration with Danny, his oldest son. Donald knew he was mortal, and thus life needed to be lived as though precious and limited. Danny thought himself immortal, thus did not see the importance of using his life wisely. Although Danny admired his father, he lacked respect for the deep moral principles Donald believed in, such as the Golden Rule: *Do unto others as you would have them do unto you.*

As noted, Deborah had three children by 1987, and Charles was studying engineering at the state university. For Charles, his father was his hero. Each week, Donald would write letters to his youngest son. The letters to Charles during his freshman year spoke of love, patience, and demanding work, at a difficult period of trying to find himself at a large university.

This principle of mutual respect extended to the precept of inclusion of all family members, so the couple invited all their children and their families to visit the three homes on the shortlist for what would be their dream home. The families included the oldest child, Deborah, now 46 years old, her husband and their three kids; Danny, 43 years old, and his wife and their two kids; and Charles, who made the Saturday trip from college.

The families convened along an old horse trail where the three old farm houses under consideration were separated by several miles. Next to the trail, now a gravel road, was a branch of the New River. The family was excited to know the possibility of a weekend get-away to have fun and enjoy the mountains.

Family time was important to Donald. The many years of caring for rental property and others' needs had deprived him of special time with his family. His hard work and time away from family had taken an emotional toll on teenager Danny, attention he needed from the World War II hero.

Donald envisioned all members of the family getting along. Though Donald was smart, he did not understand all the personalities and the nuances of family dynamics.

Nevertheless, he and Mary led their extended family down the dirt road, walking a few miles to find the old frame house with a foundation built from nearby timber and river rocks. The dilapidated two-story frame house was built in 1910 along the Virginia Creeper railway line between Horse Creek and a 2,700-foot-tall hill, a part of the Blue Ridge Mountains.

The closest town to the old frame home was Lansing, NC. In the early twentieth century, Lansing was a very busy place, primarily because of the Norfolk and Western Railroad Company (also known as the "Virginia Creeper"). Places like Todd, West Jefferson, Lansing, White Oak, and other towns nearby were regular stopping places for the train. There were some productive iron mines around Lansing that used the railroad to move ore.

The family that owned the frame house was the Millers; they raised cattle and crops. Drinking water came from a spring up the hill. Coal dust and chips were prominent in the front yard of the old cabin, as the rail bed was only five feet from the front door. There were no right-of-way safety regulations in the 1950s when the train carried coal from Damascus, Virginia, to West Jefferson, North Carolina. The railroad tracks were removed in 1977, high above Big Horse Creek, as the rail company became unprofitable. "Unprofitable" was not part of Donald's vocabulary; he had a practice of making the most out of almost nothing, including restoring a 1910 mountain home largely from materials at hand.

Donald was excited about the possibility of buying the house using cash. Donald's return on rental properties had been high, nearly 10 percent annually since the 1970s, and he now had a hefty balance of nearly $112,000.

This "cabin" was visible from the dirt road between gorgeous mountains, and one could hear the calming sound of the creek as it rushed by this 40-acre farm. Hiking, trout-fishing, and star-gazing were in the back of Donald's mind. His dream was still alive.

Finally, Donald and Mary offered to buy the buildings and the 40-acre farm for $28,000, using cash. Seven hundred dollars an acre was cheap, even in 1987.

For Danny, following in his father's footsteps meant hanging on to his father's "coattails" just long enough in hopes of acquiring his rental properties one day and eventually to be in charge of the 40-acre farm.

Danny prided himself on impressing his father; his actions bordered on narcissism. On Christmas in 1987, Danny called his family and his parents to come to his auto shop. Upon their arrival at the shop, Danny informed Charles and Donald that he had a little surprise. The garage door was lifted, and an eight-foot-diameter water wheel was presented to Donald.

"This is for you, Dad. Now 'we' have flowing water. Drink up." What appeared as a thoughtful gift, defined as something given with no expectation of a return, would one day reveal its hidden message.

CHAPTER 3

TRAGEDY STRIKES
THE FATHER

The winter of 1987 was bitterly cold. Ice covered much of the road to the mountain house. However, by the spring of 1988, Donald was heading up for some repairs and remodeling of the old house. He and Mary frequented the house every weekend from March to May; although Mary was not told of his dream, she could feel his motivation, his goals, and his dedication.

Mary was excited about the farm. She wanted to tell about it to all her friends, including her teaching school colleague, Margaret. Donald asked Mary to keep the new place quiet until they could make some much-needed repairs. Donald's rental property experience taught him that for older houses much rehab might be required, with significant cost.

Some of the repairs were mundane but quite necessary, including fixing the falling-in front porch and remodeling the front bedroom.

Donald and Mary painted the front bedroom and added a private bath. They told their friends back home their new remodeled bedroom was called "The Hilton".

The wrap-around front porch was supported by oblong stones originating from the nearby New River and Big Horse Creek. The creek contained thousands of flat stones almost perfect for building walls. However, the old frame house foundation made of flat stones from the nearby creek had settled some five inches since 1910. The settling of the foundation was due to soft soil that had not been compacted correctly when it was first constructed. To recreate a suitable base for a foundation, excavated and replaced soil should be tamped down. If it's not compacted enough, the house built on top of the soil will settle. Even if the soil is well-compacted, other construction conditions can cause house-settling problems.

The upstairs of the house was full of bats, snakes, and even leftover meats hanging from the rafters. To get to the upstairs, a narrow, short flight of steps was used. It was obvious that short folks must have lived at the home; Donald had to duck his head upon entrance to the steps. The whole old house creaked, but as Mary would maintain, "the house has character." For Donald, character was something he had learned about on the battlefield and as a property manager for low-income families.

In the spring of 1988, Donald planned a trip to the mountain house with Charles. He had spent all that Friday morning procuring lumber, nails, and other tools they would transport in the little white truck to his prize, their new family farm.

Donald believed the house was not really his, but a family place for them to enjoy the scenery and "good times." He had learned the principle of inclusion during World War II, where unselfishness meant to "be your brother's keeper."

Within fifteen minutes of Charles's arrival, Donald said, "Let's go to the mountains. Your mother will join us tomorrow."

Would "tomorrow in the mountains" come true for this dreamer, the pencil doodler as a boy, the artist, World War II soldier, the "family values" hero?

Charles was excited to take road trips with his father; such car rides with Donald were both memorable and instructional.

From opening the hood to checking the oil and even to being admonished for what Charles thought were petty little things.

Charles rolled down his window to throw out a gum wrapper to which his Dad yelled "Don't you ever throw out trash again!" Throwing out something small like a gum wrapper seemed fine with Charles but Donald had learned that cleanliness and Godliness go hand in hand. Charles' time with his mentor and father made him happy.

Not too far along the highway to the hills of North Carolina, Donald stopped to pick up a soft drink and a snack, simple pleasures of this man's modest lifestyle. As the route of the two-and-one-half-hour journey increased in elevation, so did the depth of the conversation between him and his son.

For most men who were logical, left-brain builders of things, deep conversations were not something learned or taught during the Depression or W.W. II. More superficial conversations about cars, the weather, and sports were common among most, and Donald's talking similarly did not "go deep" frequently, but for some reason, when he did do so, he revealed his feelings mostly to Charles.

Charles felt profound conversation with his father was often too complicated; his young mind had little ability to appreciate some of the finer things of life, like long hikes, the cool pure mountain air, and buffets at all-you-can-eat country stores ... and "the birds and the bees"

Nevertheless, this sunny day on their drive, Donald opened up to Charles about his dream; he gave the young lad a taste of the world's flavors Donald wanted him to share. One topic was, "If I died today, what would you want me to leave you?" Donald asked this of Charles about halfway up the rolling highway.

At this stage in Donald's life, Charles was his "pride and joy." Charles's siblings, Deborah and Danny, were jealous of this relationship despite Charles's appreciation of them.

The spring day in May of 1988 was sunny, with a

temperature of 82 degrees. The awe-inspiring hills could be seen by all who traveled along the western highway. As Donald told his son, it was an overwhelmingly joyous feeling to be going to their mountain home. The home itself, the associated carpentry work, and just spending time with his family were pleasures for Donald.

After their two-and-one-half-hour drive, Donald and Charles arrived at the old mountain house. They began to work quickly, given that at most four daylight hours were left. The house was shaded from the west by the 2700-foot mountain. Sunlight was a precious resource.

Donald told Charles to get busy repairing the front porch. It had been failing for several years; considering his thirty-nine years with Mary, he wanted her to have a solid porch to walk on.

Downstairs, the floors were coming apart, as was the foundation, originally built with large flat rocks from the creek 100 feet away. So, the vet and his younger son usually picked up these large rocks and carried them by hand to the front porch for rebuilding it.

Power tools were becoming available at the local hardware stores, but Donald was "old-school," preferring to use hand tools. Donald's drawing skills and carpentry skills enabled him to repair the porch with ease. He taught Charles as they worked together.

On this day, the large, heavy rocks proved to be too much for the father. Nevertheless, Donald was anxious to get the porch repaired. He looked forward to the next day, when he would be seeing his wife.

For Donald, tomorrow would not come.

After an hour of working on the cabin's front porch, Donald appeared unusually tired. He stopped and said, "Let's go see Bob."

They took the little white pick-up truck up the nearby mountain road; it led to Bob's place, the neighboring 30-acre farm.

On Bob's screened-in porch, Donald and Bob had a genial conversation, exchanging humorous sayings about the war, the local folk, and their construction projects. The 20-year-old Charles kept quiet, fearful of Bob's asking him some off-the-wall question or poking fun at his school smarts.

Bob, too, was working around his mountain house, fixing up several rooms and planting Christmas trees. Donald paid him $100 in cash for some tools. As Donald and Charles sat on the porch with the beautiful mountain scenery in front, Donald's complexion changed from being his natural ruddy to a whitish color. He abruptly told Bob they should be leaving.

Charles thought their break to see Bob was rather short, but he was anxious to get back to work to help his dad and in hopes of making a few extra dollars as a college student.

As Donald started back down the mountain, driving the truck, his light moments with Bob transformed to fear and pain. As Donald was driving, about a third of the way down the hill, suddenly Charles noticed his father's head sag forward, his right hand grabbing his chest, the steering wheel briefly abandoned.

Charles was not only scared but at a loss of words. He did not know what to do to help the father he so admired. Immediately, Charles knew something serious was wrong with his father. Would they both make it safely down the narrow mountain road, securely returning to the mountain house? Was his father temporarily out of breath or was something so seriously wrong they both could die on a dusty gravel mountain road so narrow that the drop-off to a much lower elevation was only three feet away?

All plans for "today" and "tomorrow with Mom" changed instantly. The man who had risked his life in war was now literally fighting the steering wheel—and the steep mountain—for his life.

Charles's left hand extended toward his father. He wanted to comfort his dad, but he also needed to grab the steering wheel of the pickup truck. Charles and his father together somehow managed to steer the truck the remaining 1/4 mile to the bottom of the mountain, where Rainbow's End Lane intersected the paved state road.

At the bottom of the mountain, Donald's head slumped all the way forward, his body became limp, and in a low, nervous voice, he whispered, "Son, I cannot make it anymore, you will need to drive. I cannot make it by myself ... I cannot steer any longer."

These emotional words let Charles know tears would suffice. He pulled the nearly lifeless, 185-pound body of his father across his lap and switched places with him. The former warrior, the dad and dreamer, was suffering a massive heart attack.

The nearest doctor was about six miles away, but upon arriving at the small country office, Charles found it closed for the day, so he drove rapidly, heading toward the nearest hospital along hilly, winding roads that kept his speed at about 40 mph.

Despite appearing lifeless for 45 minutes in the passenger seat, Donald then recovered: his pain subsided before they reached the hospital, and he even managed to walk into the Emergency Room of Jefferson Hospital. A heart attack on this beautiful day with his son was the farthest thing from Donald's mind.

At that point, Charles knew Donald's dream still existed. Charles and Donald shared their love and hopes as never before.

A particular type of heart disease, atherosclerosis, is a buildup of fat and cholesterol, plaque, formed in the arteries. A heart attack occurs when a piece of that plaque breaks off and creates a clot that blocks blood flow to the heart muscle. In fact, several years earlier, Donald had a mild heart attack, but he did not tell anyone until years later.

The classic heart attack signs are chest pain, pain or discomfort in one or both arms, the back, the shoulders, the neck, or the stomach, pain often mistaken for indigestion, accompanied by shortness of breath. Donald had experienced some of these signs before, but he preferred not to burden others, and so his condition went unchecked until that day.

According to the AARP, about every thirty-three seconds, someone in the U.S. has a heart attack. Every sixty seconds, a person dies of a heart attack. How sufferers respond in the critical first moments of a heart attack can be the difference between life and death. A person having a heart attack needs to get to the hospital within an hour to ensure the best outcome. Every second counts. The delay by Charles in transporting Donald to critical care troubled the young man.

Donald was transferred by helicopter to West Forsyth Hospital some 100 miles away. A helicopter in the rural parts of the North Carolina Mountains in 1988 traveled a speed of more than 125 mph. The cardiac damage was already done, due to a massive heart attack with no relief for one hour. For Charles, severe disappointment came when the doctors informed him that the 45-minutes' delay in receiving blood thinner might cost his father's life.

Driving the little truck, Charles followed the helicopter overhead going east until the aerial vehicle was nowhere in sight. During this two-hour trip, Charles's thoughts were of disappointment, fear, and fondness: disappointment that his father's goal to repair the home was not going to happen for an undetermined amount of time, fear that the heart attack may be severe enough to change the course of his father's life as he had known it. The sailing ship of their lives had run into a sudden storm out of nowhere to push them on a very different path.

Somehow, Charles arrived at the Forsyth Hospital before the helicopter. The scene was much like what you see in movies: the chopper landed, and his father's body was rushed to the emergency room. There were no cell phones in 1988, so Charles was surprised and thankful to see his mother and fiancée, Abigail, waiting for him. Danny was out of town, but quickly found a friend who had a private jet that flew him to the hospital.

Charles knew having a relative, partner or close friend critically ill in ICU is a crisis everyone deals with differently. For him, the possibility of losing his father made him cry; the bond they had forged was special.

The emergency room tests lasted briefly. Donald was admitted to the Intensive Care Unit. Charles's mom had been anticipating that this day would be a joyful time in the mountains; that beautiful day was a shattered dream; her world was just turned upside down.

Mary spent many hours in the ICU waiting room, befriending many people. The ICU limited the number of hours for seeing patients. Family and friends came to see Donald and her. Abigail visited many times as well. Danny's wife Martha also took Mary to and from the hospital, located about 30 minutes from Donald and Mary's primary home. Deborah also visited, but she had her own young family to care for.

The times were highly uncertain, yet the family felt a sense of unity.

The family was informed by the heart surgeon that Donald had multiple issues with his ventricular valve, an abnormality called Ventricular Septal Defect (VSD), a hole in the part of the septum that separates the ventricles. The ventricles are the lower chambers of the heart. VSD allows oxygen-rich blood to flow from the left ventricle into the right ventricle, instead of flowing out of the heart and into the aorta as it should. The surgeon said Donald would not live without having his heart repaired.

A stroke occurred while Donald was on the operating table. Thereafter, Donald would never get to speak to any of his family members and explain his dream. Only Charles and Mary already knew his dream.

Many friends and family members visited Donald, including Boyd and Billie and Bob. Mary never left Donald. Abigail was a tremendous support to her. They knew the end was coming. One day with many tubes in his body and not being able to talk, Donald lifted his hand and gave a "thumbs-up," then fell asleep for good.

After a month in the ICU, Donald's condition worsened; his body was in a vegetative state, wholly unresponsive. He was on a ventilator for about two months. Mary made the decision to take Donald off life support when the doctors gave no hope for him. Mary stated that Donald had told her that he did not want to live in a vegetative state. Even so, this warrior hero was not done. Even after the ventilator was removed, Donald lived four more days, breathing on his own, his determination surprising his family and the doctors.

On July 2, late in the evening, Mary and almost everyone else, exhausted from the experience, left the ICU to get some long-awaited sleep while Danny stayed in the ICU room.

Donald died the next day, 3 July 1988, but his dream lived on.

The funeral honored this good man, this World War II hero. The family exhibited respect and love for each other. All but Charles and Mary would know Donald's dream would need work to remain alive.

Generously and foresightedly, Donald left $15,000 to each of his children, distributed by Mary as the executor.

AFTER THE ICU

After Donald died, his wife of 39 years was devastated. Her circle of friends known through Donald became a memory. She longed to have him back. Her partner's death left a profound void and a legacy that would not be accepted by her children.

A few weeks after Donald's death, Charles asked his mother what she experienced right after Donald died. She immediately named two emotions: devastation and isolation.

Mary went on to explain to her youngest son how she had released a squealing sob and dropped to the floor after hearing her husband had passed away. "I felt as if my whole body was numb. I thought my heart had stopped beating", Mary told Charles with tears. Her worst fear had indeed become reality, her emotions surreal.

How would Mary heal from this enormous loss? She grew up with an alcoholic father who was even late to her wedding. She longed to be loved in a way her father never could provide. The sober Donald had lent a helping hand to her father and other alcoholics in the community. It was Donald who gave her special hugs, ice cream dates, trips to other states, and eventually the mountain house purchased less than one year before his death. Mary became weak and vulnerable.

The pain of losing her husband left Mary in bed for days, plagued by feelings of extreme sadness and anxiety. A spouse's death leaves emptiness hard to fill. Grieving was day after day, with no end in sight.

There was no one left in the house with whom to share the events of the day, discuss the broken pipes and unpleasant politics, relish the antics and achievements of the grandchildren; now she had lost her partner to work on the mountain house with and grow old together.

Mary missed Donald's daily company, his sharp wit, his astute commentary on the news of the day, going to church together and touring quant places in the mountains.

As for many widows of the post-WWII era, there were also practical issues that served as daily reminders of his absence. Who would open the jars that defied Mary's efforts? Who would pick up the kitchen chairs, so she could scrub the floors on her hands and knees? Who would check the oil in her car and fill the car up with gas?

Mary thought if somehow Donald had been a bad, unlikeable human being, his loss would free her to live a better life; instead, she cherished every day of the life she had experienced with him. She longed for him. She missed him.

Persevering, she learned how to navigate the world as a widow. Tasks like hanging framed paintings, picking up tree limbs and doing yard work became part of a homeowner's ritual she embraced. She slowly began to carry his dream and all her memories to the mountain house in October of 1988.

Gradually, Danny began taking a predominant, seemingly overbearing, interest in the mountain house, regularly mowing the three-acre field, updating the interior plumbing, and remodeling the kitchen. The families had once gathered to celebrate the new farm prospect, now Danny seemed to be doing all the needed chores himself without getting help and agreement from other family members.

Although it did not seem unusual for handyman Danny to want to do all the chores around the mountain house, his efforts became noticeable to his mother, but they even caused his wife to question his new time spent away from home and created some resulting strife with his immediate family.

Donald's death led his family to consider more deeply their family's values.

CHAPTER 4

FAMILY VALUES

What are family values? What did Donald and Mary view as fundamental family values? Do they originate genetically from being blood kin or are they personal relationship bonds and beliefs that link family members who share mutual respect and joy in each other's life?

Donald learned one aspect of family values from his father and mother. Donald had two siblings, but only one of them lived. Tragically, Donald's baby brother died as an infant from an aspirin overdose. Losing his baby brother evoked in him empathy and concern for others. Donald also had humility. When Donald's parents passed away, the only memento he wished for was his baby brother's piggy bank. Family values for Donald included loyalty and a mutual respect for the dignity of human life.

Donald learned another aspect of family values from his platoon during WWII. He and his comrades were honest; they made and kept promises with mutual obligations for daily survival. His friendships and loyalty were inclusive of others, trustworthy, unselfish, and giving ... with little expectation for a return on his "family values" investment.

For Donald and Mary, family values meant you have each other's back, no matter what—being there for each other when needed, not expecting anything in return. The traditional family values they knew included hard work, fairness, decency, and altruism. These values contributed to economic advantage when compared to many other struggling families.

For them, the father worked outside the home, and the mother tended to domestic matters. Families ate dinner together, prayed together, and watched television together. There were no cell phones to engross their users, and the sharing of resources was more commonplace.

Family values for Donald was sitting by the fireplace and talking with Mary, Charles, and Bob, his longtime Jaycee friend. There was television to enjoy together, but more important to Donald were good talks about past and present-day activities.

At least among members of the family, there were altruistic rather than selfish endeavors. Sadly, their children did not honor these values later in life.

Although Donald was not a deeply spiritual person, the horrors of WWII had enhanced his faith in God. His Bronze Star with "V" was an honor awarded for valor during combat actions against an enemy force. It is the fourth highest award for military combat bravery. Donald's Bronze Star was for direct fire against German soldiers during the ground assault of France in June of 1944. It was during this enemy fire that Donald asked God to protect him and his fellow squad members. Although Donald's horrific memories of the war left him speechless on many occasions, he told Charles once that he had endured enemy fire, and he suffered shrapnel wounds to his face and shoulder.

Shrapnel fragments wounded him during the military operations following his 4th Infantry Division's landing on Utah Beach on D-Day. As his division turned north toward Cherbourg, France, they ran into rough counter-fire that was to cost the division over 5,000 battle casualties in the next three weeks.

Donald explained to Charles he carried a small *Bible* in his front shirt pocket, the *Heart-Shield Bible*. The Bible was designed to fit securely into the chest pocket of a soldier's uniform. Metal plates were attached to the front cover of the *Bible* to stop a bullet from reaching the soldier's heart.

President Franklin Delano Roosevelt had announced, "We cannot read the history of our rise and development as a Nation without reckoning with the place the *Bible* has occupied in shaping the advances of the Republic. Where we have been truest and most consistent in obeying its precepts, we have attained the greatest measure of contentment and prosperity; where it has been to us as the words of a book that is sealed, we have faltered in our way, lost our range-finders, and found our progress checked. It is well that we observe this anniversary of the first publishing of our English *Bible*. The time is propitious to place a fresh emphasis upon its place and worth in the economy of our life as a people."

Donald recalled in tears how the enemy's counter-fire bullets came over him; his *Bible* stopped one of the bullets from piercing his chest. "Son, you would not be here today without that *Bible*".

So, the *Bible* and God carried a real-life lesson for Donald. The lesson was part of his dream that he wanted to leave as a legacy

He told Charles on one of their joy rides in the '76 Buick that every man should ask, "Is there a God?"

Donald believed God made Himself known through the inspired words found in the *Bible*. In the family living room, Donald kept a *Bible,* a large one handed down from previous generations.

Sadly, today marriage is dishonored by some people who want to redefine the meaning of marriage. It is dismissed as an antiquated, manmade tradition. It is even denounced in some liberal circles as an enemy of women and is demeaned in movies and television. Some of this thinking is out of fear that it will limit one's personal freedom. Instead of being honored, marriage is too often ridiculed, resented, rejected, and redefined.

As author Mario Puzo once said, "The strength of a family, like the strength of an army, is in its loyalty to each other."

While most parents may not expect or even want that their children will become carbon copies of themselves, they likely want their children to live "the good life," one full of integrity, honor, and justice. These principles were no less important to Donald and Mary. However, as will be seen, none of the children would honor their father completely by carrying on all the family values so important to Donald the patriarch. As Donald himself had shown, these values were sometimes found to be too difficult to uphold in practice.

CHAPTER 5

DEPRESSION IN THE MOTHER

After Donald died, Mary was shattered. His dream had not come true, and at least in her mind, she thought she would never see the beauty in a rainbow again. The rainbow's colors come from pure white light that the raindrops break into at least seven visual colors (red, orange, yellow, green, blue, and violet, and colors in between). Mary wanted no lessons on science, physics, or religion during this time of deep pain and grieving. She wanted to be left alone.

Few things in life are more depressing than losing a loved one. Losing her beloved spouse led to depression for Mary. She was now a senior, in her twilight years; Donald had promised a life of fun and joy in the mountains. Mary did not know how she had gotten to this place of loneliness. How had her life unraveled, leaving her sitting in a pile of used tissues, unfulfilled wishes, and hopeless dreams?

Her plans had been his plans. They were big. In one tragic heart attack, all came crashing down. This was not the life she envisioned. That was for sure.

As numerous research studies have demonstrated, bereavement by a spouse is a major source of life stress that can leave people vulnerable to later problems, including depression, chronic stress, and reduced life expectancy. It can be very difficult to cope with the destruction of our plans and dreams for the future, especially if we believed those plans had come from God in the first place. Shock, denial, confusion, anger, and even descent into depression are common reactions.

A poem by Kathy Murphy sums up the loss of a husband which Mary endured:

I sit alone now in the darkness of despair.

I cry my silent tears,

My heart is broken into a million tiny pieces.

The silence is deafening to my ears.

Mary began to stay at the mountain house by herself for many days. Her children and her old friends became concerned about her being alone so much.

CHAPTER 6

THE SECOND MARRIAGE

The devastating death of Mary's husband was a deep wound, much like the ones her beloved had suffered in World War II. However, like many Depression-Era babies, Mary's resilience and support from her immediate family and friends enabled healing of her soul.

Eventually, Mary started going back to church and socializing with close girlfriends. Not too long after her new-found church work, one of the parishioners, William, noticed this attractive sixty-year-old lady, and he pursued her. William and the minister were friends, so the gentlemanly William asked him whether Mary was single.

The minister, also a WWII veteran, responded to William that Mary had been a widow for less than one year since her first husband died. Ironically, William's previous wife, also named Mary, had died less than a year before he inquired about Mary at church. Mary was not quick to inform anyone about dating William, but their first date could not keep their fresh friendship quiet. That dinner date was planned for a town thirty minutes' drive from home, but oddly a church member was also eating at the same restaurant. The news was out: William and Mary were dating.

The primary home that Mary and Donald had shared

for almost 30 years was quiet. No children were playing. No whistles could be heard from her husband in the backyard. In Mary's mind, no other man could replace Donald and at least one of their homes was deeply special to Mary. Mary spent most of her time at the dreamer's home-away-from-home, the 40-acre farm with the mountain house next to the river.

As Mary and William began attending church together, their mutual friendship deepened. Their time with friends now included trips to the mountain house.

William took part in developments at the mountain house. He planted trees and hiked with Mary, despite his preference for the beach. William grew up in eastern North Carolina, where the BBQ is tasty and folks are down to earth. William was born in Whiteville, NC, but after the Korean War, he settled in the central part of the state to start an insurance business that prospered and was able to support enabling all five of his children to obtain college degrees.

William lifted Mary's spirits. He had a family-oriented background. With his first they had five children—three boys and two girls. By all accounts, William had a good marriage; unfortunately, his wife developed bone cancer, and he took care of her for several years before she died.

William's children included a school teacher, a lawyer, a professor, a salesman, and a retirement-home caregiver. Mary developed a fond relationship with William's oldest daughter, the retirement-home manager. Their inclinations to care for others led them to share stories and deepest emotions, including their losses, the deaths of those close to them (for example, Mary's husband, Donald, and William's wife, Mary.)

William was a traditional man. He was a veteran of World War II, having served in the U.S. Army Air Force, and he was active in the Lions Club. At church he was a well-known Sunday school teacher, one who knew his *Holy Bible* well.

William had met his first wife in eastern North Carolina before he left for boot camp. One memory he shared with his first Mary was in a letter that showed him missing home, home-cooked meals, and his girlfriend:

Dear Mary,

I'm an airman now. We got sworn in yesterday at about 4 o'clock. Outside of getting sworn in yesterday, we did nothing but play cards. We played in the morning and then in the evening.

We got so much coffee and donuts yesterday it was disgraceful. We got coffee at the bus station, coffee when we got on the bus, also when we got to Fort Bragg, then when we went to the train station. Every place we got about three candy bars too. We got razor blades, soap, cigarettes, *Bibles*, shaving cream, and all sorts of material like that.

I miss you dearly and I will write again soon.

Godspeed,
William

Upon arriving overseas, William was allowed to tell his family only that he was stationed in Italy. As they redeployed, a thunderous sky shot bullets of rain, forcing the American airmen to land in North Africa just before Christmas, 1944. William was among the young aviators destined for Europe to begin bombing missions. These plans were delayed with a brief stop in Morocco.

All in their late teens or early twenties, the young men were eager to seize upon any high jinks they could muster from this welcome delay. Officers warned the airmen that the Moroccan port city was off-limits, but the newly minted flyboys, filled with youthful spirit and bravado, ignored their commanders and poked into the city's every cranny and Kasbah. William stayed in his bunker; he was destined to be a family man, and he remembered what his mother had warned him about mischief and what the airmen were now calling "partying." In fact, William's mother was a devout Christian lady; she had taught him the verse from Matthew 7:13,14: "Enter through the narrow gate. For wide is the gate and broad is the road that leads to destruction, and many enter through it. But small is the gate and narrow the road that leads to life, and only a few find it."

During the previous year, William had been a model airman during navigator training with the U.S. Army Air Corps in Hondo, Texas, where daunting coursework, grueling tests of physical endurance, and the specter of "washing out" haunted the young cadets. Failure to measure up meant a sure ticket to the infantry. Having beaten the odds and graduated as a navigator, William was about to face combat in flak-ripped skies. He might well have been safer in the infantry.

William was a member of the 929th Bomber Squadron, 888th Bombardment Group. He and ten other airmen assigned to a B-24 Liberator aircraft left Grottaglie Army Air Base in Italy on 28 February 1945, for a mission over Italy. Their target was a railroad bridge in northern Italy, which Germany's Nazis used to move personnel and equipment out of the country.

It is estimated that between September 1943 and April 1945, some 60,000–70,000 Allied and 150,000 German soldiers died in Italy. Overall, Allied casualties during the campaign totaled about 320,000; the corresponding German figure exceeded 330,000. Fascist Italy, prior to its collapse, suffered about 200,000 casualties, mostly POWs taken in the Allied invasion of Sicily, including more than 40,000 killed or missing.

William was a part of Operation Strangle, a series of air interdiction operations by the United States Fifteenth and Twelfth Air Forces during the Italian Campaign of World War II, done to disrupt German supply routes in Italy north of Rome. It lasted from March 24, 1943, until the fall of Rome in the spring of 1944. Its aim was to prevent essential supplies from reaching German forces in central Italy and compel a German withdrawal. The strategic goal of the air assault was to eliminate or greatly reduce the need for a ground assault on the region. Although the initial goal of forcing the enemy to withdraw was not achieved, the air blockade of Operation Strangle played a significant role in the success of the subsequent ground assault.

William and his aircrew, flying from Grottaglie Army Air Base as the 888th Bombardment Group, hit the Po River bridge. Bombers like William's were easy targets, flying at relatively low 12,000 feet over the German radar-controlled anti-aircraft guns protecting the bridge. In contrast, "The Heavies," the B-17, B-24 and B-25 bombers, flew at twice that altitude to bomb their targets.

William recounted a story about the mission to future wife Mary one beautiful sunny day in North Carolina in 1990, while on his death bed with terminal cancer. He could still talk. The memory of having been near death never left him: "I was leading the group to the target when I took a hit from enemy flak and my rudder jammed. The group followed me, and we missed the target," he explained. "After I got the rudder cables unjammed, we did a 180-degree turn ten miles out, came back over the target and took it out. Our mission was completed."

William's colonel was on the flight with them that day. The colonel told him after they got out of enemy territory, "I'm putting you in for a Distinguished Flying Cross," a rare honor, given for bravery in combat.

William's principles were evident in his everyday life, even to the extent of correcting the younger generation, including Deborah and Danny's family when they forgot the values of respect and honor. Once, Deborah's husband wore his baseball cap to the dinner table at the Christmas meal. William quickly and sternly reminded this 45-year-old man to remove his cap, as a sign of respect. William's old-fashion expectations for etiquette from his family were like those of a medieval knight. A knight who failed to remove his helmet or lift his visor might suffer fatal consequences. In twentieth-century North Carolina, those consequences were not death but included family disharmony.

Despite missing Donald, Mary found that William's gentlemanly character and affectionate smiles lifted her spirits; she also liked that he was a devout Christian and a family man.

Mary's youngest son, Charles, admired William, although with some apprehension, as the loss of his father was just two years prior. Charles's emotional pain had lightened, but the memory of his father and this dreamer's dream endured.

Charles's apprehension about Mary's new friend subsided as a wedding day was set. Danny had a much different attitude, fearing William would take over his mother's estate and threaten his inheritance.

Donald had once said about Danny, "He always has to be in control."

In Danny, this impulse to control was a sign of insecurity and narcissism. Danny was a control freak. William shared much of the family values Donald had; William was a much-needed father figure for the emotionally charged Spencer family.

In 1990, Mary Spencer wed William White. Everyone called William "WW" or "Double," for short. WW took Mary to Niagara Falls and then to New England.

Life for Mary was exciting and adventurous, fun-filled for the next few years. They went on vacations to Alaska and Montana. William's love for her grew, as did the acceptance among family members of the new relationship.

In 1995, William, Mary, and Charles's family took a short vacation to the beach where Mary and William owned a "time share," a beach-front condo. Charles and wife Abigail had a new son, Bradley, then two years old. They left their Raleigh,

NC, apartment to meet William and Mary at the beach. William grew up in Eastern North Carolina; he often visited the beach and enjoyed the sun. The families spent the day on the beach, enjoying sun and sand.

Mary noticed an abnormal mole on William's back; he had not seen this mole before. Over the next few months, the mole turned very dark, grew, and started to itch.

Mary insisted William go to the dermatologist and get it checked out. William did so and ended up walking out of the dermatologist's office thinking, *all is well; glad that's over.* The doctor said he would see William again in a year. Surprisingly, a couple of days later, William got a call from someone at the dermatologist's office saying he needed to come in ASAP, but they couldn't tell him why.

Mary had endured three months of the ICU with Donald, and his death had brought deep emotional pain. Regarding William, she hoped that the dermatologist phone call would not be any shocking news. While Mary worked to keep William's five- bedroom brick home clean and warm, her domestic duties did not keep her from worrying all day about William as he went to the dermatologist for the biopsy report.

The drive home for William from the dermatologist was deeply disappointing. He had to tell Mary the mole she had discovered was cancerous.

William pondered, *I have cancer, and I am only 70 years old. How did this happen? Am I not invincible!?*

Like most sun-lovers, William had a preconceived notion of skin cancer, diminishing its threat, and like most, he could not have been more wrong. William had no idea how serious melanoma was. He certainly didn't think he could get it just because he had often visited the beach as a boy and throughout his first marriage.

Upon hearing the diagnosis of melanoma from William, Mary was devastated.

It was recommended that William began taking Interferon, a new, experimental, controversial drug for cancer treatment.

The use of Interferon can lead to high fever, joint pain, alopecia (baldness), loss of appetite, anorexia, nagging headache, fatigue, depression, and an injured thyroid.

All cancer is terrible, and melanoma especially terrible, one of the deadliest cancers. It spreads quickly from your skin to your internal organs. Few drugs can stop it. It doesn't discriminate by age and is one of the most common cancers for those under 30. For those young folks reading this book, please know how important it is to check your skin...detecting melanoma early is the key.

Several patients taking the cancer-fighting Interferon noted that they should have quit the drug after a few months, due to the adverse, painful side effects. These patients became progressively worse from around month 6 and had little energy. Some could not walk around the block, had to quit driving, and would cough until they could barely breathe. These reactions happened to William. Mary stayed by his side day and night.

William developed several infections in his lymph nodes. The doctors also removed a tumor from one of his lymph nodes. The cancer was aggressive.

Mary and William liked to sit by the fireplace at his home and tell stories or entertain their children. As they shared stories one night, William coughed, and blood came from his mouth. Mary knew her husband's cancer was very serious, and his time was limited. Both Mary and William were dejected.

How will I endure another emotional trauma? Mary thought.

Mary found her strength within her soul.

William was not afraid to die. On his death bed, he told Mary lovingly, "I am not afraid to die; I just do not want to leave you."

William had a true love for Mary. Was their falling in love a random event or designed by Divine intervention? After all, both had previously endured hardships and now were special to each other—a blessing for those who believed in God's active shaping of human destinies.

The last shower William took, he turned on the cold-water faucet and left the hot water off. Why? Because he wanted to be thankful for the hot water. By feeling only the cold water, he practiced the "family value" of thankfulness.

William died with Mary and one of his daughters, Kay, present.

CHAPTER 7

NO PROPOSAL
FOR THE MOTHER

When a woman experiences two good marriages, her natural reaction can include the desire for another good
marriage. Some marriage counselors say that it should be at
least a year after the death of your spouse before you make
any major decision. This certainly includes marriage.

If the death of a mate was sudden, the resolution of grief
may be particularly difficult. Such was the case with Mary.
Furthermore, some counselors recommend waiting several years before even considering the idea of remarriage.
Conversely, if your mate had a lingering illness and the grief
process was substantial before his or her death, the widow may
be comfortable in remarrying in less than a year. For Mary the
timing to be introduced to Morris could not have been better,
at least in her mind.

If Mary's new friend had children, how would Deborah,
Danny, and Charles feel about another marriage for the
widow?

This issue was a serious one for Mary's three children.
Her children did not know Morris, and they had lost their
father Donald in 1988, and now less than one year earlier,

William had died. Introducing a new man into the family's get-togethers would be hard. On top of that, Danny wanted to take over his mother's affairs, and any man she dated or married would be a threat to him.

MORRIS

Mary was quickly set up with Morris by a close friend who lived in the mountains near the family farm. Morris was a widower.

Morris had four children from his only marriage—two boys and two girls. His wife died of excessive tobacco smoking; her demise left Morris lonely.

What attracted Mary to Morris was that he was friendly and outgoing. He owned homes in Ashe County as well as in the Piedmont, similar to her own housing situation. He also was a native of the mountains and his knowing the area and the local folks helped rekindle in Mary her love for the mountain house.

Mary met Morris through a mutual friend in the mountain community. Morris was born in Ashe County and went on to work for the FBI, living in the District of Columbia while traveling the states investigating the Mafia and other bad guys.

Charles and Morris had a shallow relationship, partly due to Charles's lack of trust of a new partner for Mary after the death of William.

One afternoon in Jefferson, Charles observed that Morris had a gun discreetly holstered beneath the waistband of his pants. Charles asked him about it. During his 27 years as a "fed," Morris explained, he was often concerned for his life. As he recalled, "I hung out with Mafia-made guys who kill undercovers like me."

He and Mary spent much time together, but others questioned whether it was really quality time, time that included words of mutual affirmation and affection.

THE BAPTISM

Mary and her daughter's family decided to take a trip with their church to the Holy Land. So, Mary invited Morris to go along with her, Deborah, and her husband, a well-educated Baptist preacher. The trip was educational, a success, due in part to Mary's experience traveling in prior years with Donald to Europe and with William across the United States.

The trip was special for Mary because of its spiritual over-tones. Her devastating loss of two dearly beloved husbands made her reflect deeply on family and her dream, which had been passed on to her from Donald. Although she loved the deceased William, it was Donald's dream she would carry in her heart on the trip.

Mary rode a camel, viewed the Dead Sea, and was baptized in the Jordan River, brought to the water by Deborah's hus-band, John, an educated preacher.

For some, baptism is only symbolic, but on this day Mary was touched "by the hand of God," or, as Charles told her dur-ing her healing from Donald's death, "You received Divine intervention."

In Israel, while among her daughter and some grandchil-dren, she was asked by the preacher why she wanted to be pu-rified. Why would Mary want to be purified when she had not been committing sin by all accounts? This widow twice-over was seeking God's redemptive power. After the deep pain she experienced from the loss of Donald and William, she prayed for healing of her heart.

Then the preacher led Mary to the Jordan. The Jordan River may look like a typical river of the Middle East, but the symbolism of it is incomparable to other locations as to the spiritual experience for those seeking to be cleansed.

According to the Christian teachings, the Jordan River is considered the third most holy site in the Holy Land, just af-ter His birthplace, the Nativity Grotto in Bethlehem, and the crucifixion site, Golgotha, in Jerusalem. The Jordan River is the site of the very important event of Jesus' life—His baptism and beginning of His ministry.

It was John the Baptist who decided to baptize people in the Jordan River. Many scholars think that he might have been influenced by the Essenes, who, like John, were leading an ascetic life in the wilderness of Qumran or Israel's Ein Gedi. One of their principal religious rituals was a daily immersion in water to regain purity.

Baptism with water, practiced since the beginning of the Church, represents admission into the Christian community and is essential for salvation. "Truly, truly, I say to you, unless one is born of water and the Spirit, he cannot enter into the Kingdom of God" (*John* 3:5).

In Christianity, baptism is a sign of "repentance and forgiveness of sins" (*Mark* 1:4) and the beginning of the life in Christ within the Church. Christians are baptized in the name of the triune God: "the Father, and the Son and the Holy Spirit" (*Matthew* 28:19).

Through baptism, Christians connect with the death, burial, and resurrection of Jesus: "And this water symbolizes baptism that now saves you [...] by the resurrection of Jesus Christ" (*1 Peter* 3:21).

This preacher had baptized many before Mary in his years of ministry. In his heart this time was special for him, as Mary and several others would commit to or rededicate their life to God.

All of Mary's emotional pain came to a head, her grief from losing her husband to her alcoholic father was met by the presence of The Almighty, His unfailing love, flowing along the river Jordan where the Apostle Paul baptized Jesus Christ. She could hear the preacher's words quoting the Bible (John 3:15): "I tell you the truth, no one can enter the kingdom of God unless he is born of water and the Spirit." (NIV)

Like the song by Carrie Underwood, "Something in the Water," Mary followed the preacher down to the river.

Although her heart was not dirty, she wanted to be clean like Jesus. In that moment of repentance and sorrow she was changed, forever. And she was stronger. For Mary, there must have been "something in the water".

Mary had attended a Methodist Church most of her life; the ritual for cleansing the soul was by sprinkling water on a child's head. But in Israel, she was inspired by the *Bible,* as read by the tour guide along the Jordan, specifically that Jesus Christ was baptized by John the Baptist as an act of obedience to God, the heavenly Father.

On this day where the Spirit was moving, words seemed insignificant. Nevertheless, the preacher man had to say something. There is no mention of a ritualistic statement, "Jesus is Lord," by the one being baptized, but this does not prove it was not done. By the second century, from writings by Tertullian and Hippolytus, we know that the one baptized was immersed three times in the name of the Father, Son, and Holy Spirit, as well as being anointed with oil to receive the Holy Spirit.

The old Roman standard showed the person to be baptized confirming doctrines about Jesus being the Son of God and affirming the resurrection of Jesus before baptism. This was not a uniform practice in the church in the second century, but the formula was used in many churches.

The preacher, dressed in a white robe, in water up to his waist, lifted his hand to the sky and said, "Jesus is Lord."

Then, he immersed little Mary, the 70-year-old widow-twice-over, under the Jordan and brought her back up.

Mary wept with tears of joy and said, "Thank you, God."

There is something humble about the words "thank you." There is a difference between gratitude and thanksgiving. Gratitude is a feeling; thanksgiving is more of an action. Mary believed in God, based on the historicity of Jesus Christ; since she was acting on Jesus' example of baptism and His words, she was grateful.

Mary would later write in her journal, while dying of multiple myeloma, the following:

God has not promised skies always blue,

Flowers strewn pathways all our lives through.

God has not promised sun without rain,

Joy without sorrow,

Peace without pain,

But God has promised

Strength for the day,

Rest for the laborer,

Light on the way,

Grace for the trials,

Help from above,

Unfailing sympathy,

Undying love.

[Hymn, "God Hath Not Promised," lyrics by Annie Johnson Flint]

The above poem suggests that in Mary's deepest moments, poetry gave her comfort and hope, and Donald's dream still lived.

Mary's companion, Morris, was also baptized. His response was stillness and silence, no words, no non-verbal clues. No one will ever know what he truly experienced by his baptism, its true meaning to be held between him and God.

In 2000, Morris had a heart attack while he and Mary were driving from Winston-Salem to Jefferson. The visit to

Mary's home was somewhat symbolic. Morris was involved with Mary's family, although his commitment to her family's values and their original ideals was lacking.

Marriage counselors will tell you a successful or fruitful relationship is based on being unselfish. The principle of unselfishness is nothing new or extraordinary, in theory at least. A relationship cannot grow without each person's putting "energy" into each other. Like an apple that has been picked to eat and is sitting unused, if you do not put it in the refrigerator, it will rot.

Morris was not thinking about nurturing apples or putting energy into a demanding relationship. He preferred golf and fishing more than deep talks with Mary, who enjoyed profound talks about life, the mountains, and family. Morris was not interested in these. Morris wanted his independence. Instead of letting Mary go gracefully, he distanced himself from her.

Mary was outside the mountain cabin. She could hear the water flowing, which reminded her of the Jordan. The crows were calling each other, and the deer camped out in the fields. She was "in her element" that day, planting, reading, and writing, anticipating some time with Morris.

Gardening for Mary was both therapeutic and inspirational. Her wounded soul from losing her longtime husband and being dumped by Morris gave her motivation to observe nature - the mountains, tall oak trees, purple rhododendrons and other wildflowers in the river valley alongside her old cabin.

She gardened for herself and in memory of Donald, a way to carry on his dream. Her garden was unlike her childhood garden that was dead due to family strife. Her garden was manicured

Just like Zac Brown's song "Grandma's Garden" , Mary had a garden in her backyard. She had a newfound interest in seeing things grow, not die. She grew tired of death and broken relationships.

She loved to watch the seeds she planted and see things grow. But down deep she was thinking about doing what grandma does best – seeing her family grow. The 'weeds' were not brown grass but conflicts she liked to mediate and make right. Then when her family was peaceful, when her children were successful, it was her garden and her garden would grow up strong. But she knew for one child, the hoeing would be a long hard path knowing that child had too many weeds and making the row straight would be hard.

As was true of her gardening, Mary would give her love to her family, carrying on Donald's dream; sadly, the family would not appreciate it, as will be shown.

Mary was reading *Chicken Soup for the Soul,* which was quite apropos and inspiring both for her life's disappointments and for her newly found spiritual experience in Israel.

That day, Mary's soul was meeting the soil. She was a grandmother with her hoe in the soil, and she was happy. Her hair was almost gray, flowing in the mountain breeze, while she was planting lilies and daisies, and thinking of her children, Charles, Danny, and Deborah. She would also think about her seven grandchildren and who they would become and their marriage partners.

Mary wrote in her journal, reflecting on the soil, love and troubles: "You can take troubles with you, when you go to work in the garden; but you cannot bring them back. You will always bury them there."

She always worried about Danny. Danny and Mary's relationship was built on stressful emotional interactions and, to a lesser extent, on bargaining deeds, more than on deep love. Deborah would periodically call and check on Mary, mostly following up on her well-being after the Israel trip. Charles loved his mother; she was his last deep tie to his father.

Then one day, the phone rang and rang. Mary was in the flower garden next to the rustic cabin. She did not have a cell phone and those devices did not have coverage in such a remote location. She stopped planting daisies and hurried to answer the phone now ringing endlessly.

"Hello, can I help you?" Mary asked.

"This is Morris. I ain't coming up to the mountains, and I won't be back anymore."

Mary, a tough lady raised by an alcoholic father, was a strong woman who worked in inner city schools, yet she had a tender heart. She thought Morris's comments were a joke, as his dry humor was commonplace.

"What do you mean"? Mary asked.

Morris had been seeing another woman, and he said it would be better not to see Mary anymore. He said he did not feel the same way toward her as she did toward him.

This was shocking news. Mary was used to being adored and pampered by Donald and then William, men from the "greatest generation."

The men in her life had pursued her, and she had never been rejected or turned down, probably because she was a beautiful, brown-eyed, loving, supportive lady, "wife-material" ten times over.

Yet Morris had dumped Mary.

Mary was hurt. She decided to act. She obtained cosmetic surgery, a face lift.

Danny and Deborah had never liked Morris. He was not Donald, their birth father, and he was not William, whom they had grown to like, but who died before deep relationships could form among all the family members.

Danny was glad Morris was out of the picture. Like William, Morris was an impediment to controlling the Spencer Estate— the mountain farm and all of the rental property

Meanwhile, Charles thrived as a father of three, including a new baby daughter, April. Certainly, his family was unified, his career continued to grow, and Abigail remained steadfast in her support and sacrifice for Charles and their family.

CHAPTER 8

ASIA BUSINESS

In fall 2003, Charles began a new position as Sr. Engineer with the Skywire Engineering Company. Skywire was a growing manufacturer of cellular phone components; the customers were mostly headquartered in Asia.

Charles's job was to provide technical solutions to support large customers manufacturing phones in factories in Asia. He was considered a Sales Engineer to the U.S.-based team and an expert in cell phone components to the Japanese and Chinese sales teams.

Charles was a learner. He had decided that education would help propel his career even if a poor economy set in. But he knew a piece of paper (such as a graduate degree diploma) meant little unless it could be applied in a fast-growing technological economy.

His goal was to learn more about wireless communications and create novel cell phone devices and achieve recognition and share information by publishing papers.

The job with Skywire included laboratory experiments and frequent travel to Asia, especially Japan. Skywire's sales efforts were focused on the big Japanese telecom firms who were buying components from Chinese makers. Japanese demands for high-quality components were rooted in the

Deming philosophy of statistical quality control, an approach unfortunately initially rejected by the U.S. manufacturers during World War II, but subsequently adopted decades later.

Charles's appreciation and enjoyment of hands-on work at Skywire came from his boyhood tinkering with shortwave radio circuits and antennas. As a boy, he built a crystal radio detector from ordinary home supplies, and then he climbed a tree to place a wire antenna for reception.

Charles did not shy away from the opportunity to travel overseas. As a young boy, his mother took him on frequent trips around the Western Hemisphere. He knew travel offered cultural experiences no textbook could provide.

Charles was also adventurous.

Meanwhile, Abigail was tending to their children. She also worked part-time as a dental hygienist two days per week.

Japanese business customs among men (most business there is done by men) include a special appreciation for the business card, a formal meeting agenda, and lots of sushi, alcohol, dinners, and hostess bars.

A hostess bar offered a new and exciting atmosphere for Charles, especially in the elite province of Ginza, a 10-block area of Tokyo that is full of upscale shopping centers, grand restaurants, and high-end fashion stores.

Come nighttime, the bustling hostess district of Ginza is packed with an after-work crowd of men and women who spill out onto the street amid bright neon signs advertising diverse types of hostess bars. Young women wait outside these bars, trying to attract new customers.

Probably the most common reason that a woman chooses to hostess is the money. In Japanese clubs, these women can make from ¥3,000 to ¥5,000 per hour on average (that is about $30 to $50 per hour). Their pay is sometimes more, sometimes less, depending on the club and how good that hostess is at her job. In Japan, where a glass ceiling still exists for women in the workplace, an average working woman with a day job is an office worker or secretary who still must buy her boss chocolates on Valentine's Day and make the staff tea.

Japanese businessmen would pay extra simply for a hostess to sit and talk with them. The hostesses were dressed in low-cut tight dresses and were smiling from ear to ear. Rarely would the hostess offer private time or sex. Charles knew this was not the kind of place that would enhance family values, but the sushi, alcohol, and attention were tempting. Charles thought his business success depended on participating in it.

Charles would later regret going to the hostess bars with his Japanese colleagues rather than staying in his hotel room.

For Charles, the new cultural experience was intellectually inspiring. He had never traveled to Asia, but he was ready to experience new things in life.

He had only heard about Japan from studying Pearl Harbor and Hiroshima in World War II in high school. He was also anxious that much of the work to be done in Japan would depend on his technical skills to demonstrate new products to very demanding businessmen.

On Charles's first trip to Japan, he came with his supervisor, Jeremy. Jeremy was a strict leader in business and in his personal life. Jeremy gave Charles some tips on travel, including enduring the long, thirteen-hour flight, security measures at Narita Airport, and Japanese food.

On this trip, they would visit customers in Tokyo, Osaka, and Hiroshima. Jeremy would provide Charles support in the meetings and then return to his own hotel room.

Charles wanted adventure. Jeremy wanted sleep. Charles wanted to see first-hand some of the cultural differences in Japan, and so he sought out travel guides on the weekend. Japan is a country Charles only dreamed about visiting. As a sixteen-year-old, he had found that his ham radio hobby introduced him to a Japanese student who lived in Tokyo. Charles met the man by Morse code radio transmission between Piedmont, NC, and downtown Tokyo. Charles was always fascinated with people and places; the geography and culture of Japan fit the bill.

Flying into Tokyo, Charles viewed the incredible mountain scenery, as well as one of the world's most chaotic and quirky cities (Tokyo), a city which has a long history of culture and tradition, and incredible cuisine with authentic sushi on every corner.

Jeremy and Charles arrived Tuesday to Narita Airport and got through customs and immigration. "Japan is US-friendly; don't forget we helped them rebuild their country after World War II", Charles asserted to Jeremy. But unlike the United States, Japan is very strict on immigration. The country has remained relatively closed to foreigners, who make up only two percent of the population of 127 million. Yet, Japan is especially short of workers. Fully eighty-three percent of firms have trouble hiring, according to Manpower, a recruiting firm, and this figure is the highest of any country it surveys.

Charles and Jeremy would meet with some large cell-phone makers. The trip was spread out over two weeks, giving Charles the weekend in between to venture out.

Most travel experts advise us to travel to foreign places in pairs. Jeremy was not interested in sushi or the "bullet train," but Charles was so interested that he planned a trip to Hiroshima from Tokyo. It was a Saturday morning, and the jet lag had worn off.

After an eventful five-day stay in Tokyo, Charles caught the bullet train and travelled four hours south of Tokyo to Hiroshima. To be frank, Charles enjoyed Tokyo, but he was glad to be leaving the hustle and bustle of the world's most populous city for somewhere a little bit quieter.

The "bullet train" is actually called the "Shinkansen" by the natives of Japan. The Shinkansen is a high-speed railway line consisting of over 1,700 miles of lines with maximum speeds of 150 to 200 mph.

Being an engineer, Charles was fascinated with the Shinkansen's design and operation. Since the mass transportation network in the United States is still somewhat lacking, the extensive network in Japan was overwhelming.

The Shinkansen uses a 25,000-volt alternating current (AC) overhead power supply, providing more magnetic energy than the standard Japan railway electrification of the 1,500-volt direct current (DC). Power is distributed along the axles of the train to reduce the heavy axle loads.

Traveling by the Shinkansen from Tokyo to Osaka produces only around fifteen percent of the carbon dioxide of the equivalent journey by car, a saving a lot of CO_2 annually.

What Charles liked about the Shinkansen was the food, the seating, and the window views of the Japan countryside, mountains, and beaches.

Unlike the often-lackluster customer service found in trains in the U.S., the bullet train stewards were attentive, punctual, and informative.

Charles admired the countryside on his way to Hiroshima, with views of blossoming cherry trees, beaches, hand-crafted bungalows, Mount Fuji, and he enjoyed the sushi boxes.

Bento boxes were crafted specifically for travelers on the country's Shinkansen. Filling, yet not fattening like American fast food, their protein and taste Charles had learned to enjoy. The bento box presentation was almost as good as the meal: a colorful yellow egg tucked next to pink sushi or sashimi and bright-green beans and pickled ginger.

Hiroshima is a beautiful green and modern city, with numerous branches of the Ota River running through the city. However, Hiroshima is known for its much darker past of being the place where nuclear weapons were first used in warfare.

On August 6, 1945, at 8.15 a.m., the U.S. dropped "Little Boy" on Hiroshima. 80,000 people died instantly. The total amount of deaths connected to the bombing is 292,325, due to many fatally wounded dying later and deaths due to radiation sickness in the months and years following. Some U.S. military experts had maintained that an assault on the

Japanese mainland would have caused many more deaths. When this bombing was followed soon by another atomic attack at Nagasaki, the Japanese government surrendered.

The main attraction in Hiroshima is the "A-bomb Dome," the only building near the city center left standing, now a World Heritage Site. Charles thought the Dome was a good analogy of the Japanese people because even after being nuked, fire-bombed, hit by tsunamis, and having power plant meltdowns, they were still standing and just getting on with life.

What was sad were the crying Japanese children and grandchildren of lost loved ones at Hiroshima.

Charles thought to himself: *Don't the Japanese hate the U.S. for bombing Hiroshima? Why have the Japanese been so accommodating and respectful toward me?*

In spite of receiving such a terrible blow at the hands of the Americans, Japan is on friendly terms with the United States both socially and politically. Charles learned from talking to some Japanese colleagues, that showing forgiveness and kindness toward the U.S. by Japan is not considered weak. This attitude was one of many about which Charles was enlightened by in his travels in Asia.

KARAOKE WOMAN

Charles travelled to Japan almost monthly in 2005. He was introduced to a work colleague, Michael, an American-born salesman from Kansas whose wife and two children still lived in Kansas despite his Japanese citizenship.

Michael was an engineer turned salesman. He dreamed of being a rock star, which never worked out, and his move to Japan fed his ego, as he liked being a minority man gaining attention from the natives, especially the women. He managed to have fun in Japan, lots of it, make friends, fall in love, and sell stocks.

Japan is a tough country to live and work in, and Michael told Charles horror stories of businessmen working themselves to death, and how the suicide rate is shockingly high.

Compared to the average U.S. lifestyle, in Japan the pay can be low, and rent is high, especially in Tokyo. For foreigners, customs are difficult to abide by and some of which are seemingly backwards at times. To a Westerner, the stereotype is that the foreigner will never fit in, but remain a *gaijin*, Japanese for "outsider." But Michael told Charles that being adventurous, open-minded, and most of all, tolerant and understanding, he found moving to Japan one of the best decision he ever made. Charles would privately consider long-term living in Japan before his venture would come to a halt.

Michael, now forty and living permanently in Japan, was still trying to decide what he wanted to be ... at the emotional expense of his family back in Kansas. Michael's attitude and lifestyle began rubbing off on Charles.

Michael also liked hostess bars and the cheaper karaoke bars.

Roppongi is a province of Tokyo next to Ginza. As Ginza is for the rich, Roppongi is for the young and energetic crowd and the thirty-somethings who like drinking and music. Roppongi is known for its nightlife, attracting off-duty servicemen, students, and business professionals. With much illicit activity at night in Roppongi, the U. S. Embassy in Japan warned Americans to avoid the bars and clubs in Roppongi, due to increase in the reports of drug-mixed beverages.

Michael and Charles decided to bar-hop one night after meeting with several key customers and making a $1million sale with a Japanese cell phone maker Janyo.

First, Michael suggested they grab some sushi. It was already 9 p.m., and they took the rail train from Yokohama to Tokyo.

Michael picked a unique sushi restaurant with seats and a bar, but the place was not a typical sushi bar you would see in the United States. The sushi was presented on a conveyor belt at eye level while both men sat at a bar.

The place was a diner for sushi with a food cars moving

on a food track around the bar which ironically you could see the nearby train in a profecture of Tokyo. When they arrived at the restaurant, it was late for Charles, about 10 p.m. But Charles was fascinated with the food and culture. "This is a cool place", he told Michael.There were some other Japanese people inside who were finishing up. Charles and Michael ordered quickly and probably ordered too much, as they were starving. A quick meal turned into the next event, a karaoke bar crawl.

Among four or five bars on the same block visible through a light rainfall, neon lights, and emitting the sounds of the 80s, the karaoke bar Gas Panic was the bar chosen.

Michael entered the bar first. The bar was packed with men and women, Asian women. Michael was experienced with the bar scene, using pick-up lines and flirting with several Chinese women. With the music blasting, Charles was troubled by the inability to hear anyone talking.

Charles carried an English-Japanese dictionary, and he thought self-study could be put into practice at the karaoke bar. Charles and a short attractive Asian lady made eye contact immediately at the bar. Charles wearing his wedding band and dressed in a suit then greeted her: "Konnichiwa!" The lady's name was Maria and she then spoke English to Charles. With a big smile she said "You don't have to speak Japanese to me. Are you in the military?" Most of the natives, except for Maria, just laughed at him when he attempted to speak Japanese.

Maria was a Philippine-born nanny for the CEO of Nippon, Japan's telephone company. Maria and Charles swapped emails and he visited her at the Tokyo mansion of the CEO. Charles explained to Maria he was married, and their relationship went from attraction to being just friends.

When Charles arrived home after his 10-day business trip to Japan, he was eager to tell Abigail about the trip. Charles missed his children and was reminded by a recent reading the importance of appreciating his family.

Charles knew he might come to regret so much travel and

being away from his family, especially his two young girls. If one could relive one moment over and over again, what would it be? For Charles, he would later declare: "I would come home and open the door and my two daughters would scream, 'Daddy!'"

He made multiple trips to Japan, South Korea, Singapore, China, Hong Kong, and Taiwan. Each month, Charles would travel to these Asian countries to support the sales teams and their efforts to expand the cell-phone business.

Meanwhile Mary was trying to carry out Donald's dream.

CHAPTER 9

MARY'S THIRD MARRIAGE

In the fifteenth century, the kings of England remarried after divorces, beheadings, and spontaneous deaths. The fates of the wives of Henry VIII, the brutish philanderer whose divorces caused a seismic split with the Catholic Church, were grim.

Today, women don't face a death sentence in marriage, but often their reputations are on the line if they have more than one husband. Though kings and celebrities often count brides as assets, women are more likely to be stigmatized after several trips to the altar.

Serial monogamy is not our norm. U.S. Census surveys show that only four percent of men and women marry more than three times, compared with thirteen percent of men and fourteen percent of women who marry twice. So, a third marriage for Mary would be an exception, not just for statistics, but for two of her children, Danny and Deborah, who raged against her re-marrying. But why?

In a 2005 "State of Our Unions" report, Rutgers University published *The National Marriage Project,* which concluded that in the U.S. divorce was no longer a taboo. But, relationship experts say, the age-old double standard still applies when it comes to the sexes. Today it is still marginally acceptable to question, especially with regard to a woman, "How many marriages can you have and come out in one piece?"

Mary desired to stay married to one man. She had a deep desire for a companion. But this was not her fate.

Surveys of married couples suggest men and women have different views of marriage: women go into marriage for the marriage; men go into marriage for the woman.

For Mary, marriage was a wonderful journey with Donald for 39 years starting as a 19-year-old bride to the World War II hero, and later for five years to the man of her dreams, William.

Today dating agencies talk about finding a 'soul mate', a misunderstood phrase since the word soul is actually reserved for the supernatural spiritual entity and associated relationship between God and (wo)man, not for a dating acomplishment. Mary never aimed at finding a soul mate because marriage for her was a deep longing for a relationship in which to give love and be loved. She was dedicated to her husband even when he fell short, even when his moral compass went awry.

Mary wanted to be loved and to love her husband and family. After all, her birth family had been broken: her alcoholic father was even late to her wedding.

After William died, Mary met Morris, but he ultimately dumped her. Mary had never been dumped before. Her family was a bit surprised by Morris's boldness to reject the widow. Surely, Mary did like Morris, but she had not confided in him her emotions nor committed herself to him. Thus, the break-up was somewhat expected. In fact, it was a relief for her children and their families.

Although Danny and Deborah were in their forties and fifties then, they expected the marital stability they had seen in their father, Donald.

Psychologists now believe a growing body of evidence demonstrates that stressful childhood experiences have long-term negative effects on children's health and well-being through their adult years. Psychologists also believe, and common sense conveys, children tend to do best in stable households, where they know what to expect and their relationships, health, and safety are basically secure. This seems to apply to the adult children of Mary, although as adults they would seem less likely to be as affected as they would be if the events occurred when they were children.

Undergoing repeated transitions, like multiple marriages of their mother, can cause stress, threatening their emotional attachment to Mom. Such transitions might to a lesser extent affect their mental health. At the very least, the introduction of a new family member (and his family, as in-laws) can complicate relationships as well as enrich them.

In the fall of 2000, Mary decided to take a plane trip from North Carolina to Florida to see her Aunt Jackie, who was the baby sister to Mary's mother and Mary's confidante on many issues, including marriage. Jackie understood Mary because she too was married three times. Jackie and her third husband, Tony, spent much leisure time with Donald, and then William, traveling by car and boat to various getaways.

Thus, Mary looked forward to the sunny-day plane trip to the warm climate of South Florida, where Jackie and Tony made their winter home. Mary was fond of Tony, a retired New York City plumber, a jovial man who liked to play pool.

Despite the stereotype that folks from the Big Apple are crude, Tony was a soft-spoken, kind man; he fit in well with Mary's warm, Southern hospitality. Jackie was born a Southerner, but in the 1950s she moved to Manhattan to seek the glamorous city life, becoming a salesperson for Macy's. Jackie was an attractive lady, tall and curvy. Tony was a short, stocky man. Initially, one might find their appearance together rather incongruous, but after spending time with them, one could see that their love surrounded each other.

Mary's plane trip to Florida was uneventful. She brought along a novel to read. The passing of William a few years prior had freed more time to explore the mountains and now Florida. Mary was a cheerful person: furthermore, she was entering a phase in her life full of love for her grandchildren. Charles's children were thirteen and eleven, and his youngest, April, had been recently born.

Yet, Mary still deeply missed having a partner at home.

A fateful meeting soon developed. The plane's boarding was delayed and Mary's phone died before she could notify one of her children (usually she would call Charles or Danny) that her flight was now taking off later than usual. In line next to her was a friendly young lady who offered her phone for the older attractive Mary. The younger lady named Julie started a conversation with Mary before the boarding began. "This darn phone – I am going to throw it away!" Mary shouted. The whole airport could have heard her.

The plane's boarding took place as usual, except that Mary was not so familiar with the cramped seating and bag maneuvering. The flight attendant helped the aging Mary to her seat. A few minutes passed. Another boarding passenger asked Mary to change her seat. Mary had sat in the wrong seat, confused by the signage.

Mary moved back one seat, sitting next to a dark-haired lady who looked to be in her thirties. Mary started reading her book, but this lady was in a talking mood. She reminded Mary of one of her family members. Friendly Mary immediately struck up a conversation with this young woman, Julie, who lived alone in Fort Lauderdale, FL.

"Hey, nice to meet you. I've got a friend I should introduce you to" exclaimed Julie.

Julie and Mary's conversation led to subsequent phone calls between Florida and North Carolina. Then Julie phoned Mary to tell her about Asher, a recent widower, then eighty-five years old. Mary initially thought that a man eighty-five years old was not for her to consider for meeting or dating. "He's is kind of old for me, but tell me more", she asked Julie.

ASHER

Asher Anderson's story starts in Philadelphia in 1910. He was born to a boat builder. His childhood was spent walking and playing along the cobblestones of North Lindenwood Street in South Philadelphia. When Asher was only six, his father drove him and his sister in a Model A Ford station wagon bound for the shores of Delaware.

Delaware would be where Asher learned about the ocean and boat-building. Eventually, Asher found his satisfaction in the warm climate and real estate ventures in Florida's Fort Lauderdale, where he and his first wife, Dorothy, came to reside for forty-five years until her death in 1998. Fort Lauderdale is well known as a luxurious anchor for jet-setting and refined retirement.

At first, Asher and Mary corresponded by letter. Being eighty-five years old, he was meticulous and slow about his personal affairs, including writing letters. Mary, on the other hand, wanted information quickly. She asked Asher for a picture of himself.

Asher sent Mary a letter that included a picture of himself as a boy in Delaware. The boyhood picture amused Mary; she knew Asher had a fun side to him.

Dating for the average eighty-five-year-old man would usually be tranquil and uneventful. However, Asher was a youthful eighty-five-year-old, having been fortunate to live in the warm climate of Florida and having enjoyed a very successful real estate business. His health was good despite a few typical aches and pains. Asher liked to enjoy a strong drink ... but only one! It would likely be Jim Beam whiskey on the rocks. His afternoon break was whiskey and Wall Street....

Asher decided to drive his small RV from Fort Lauderdale to see Mary in North Carolina. One must give Asher credit for taking on a thirteen-hour trip by himself in a small RV at his age.

Asher enjoyed being able to drive himself around Florida.

Driving gave him a sense of freedom and accomplishment since he was losing some other abilities due to the aging process. He was actually blind in one eye due to glaucoma. However, the State of Florida was lenient on driving requirements, and he somehow always passed the test.

The courtship lasted from March to October, and it included Mary's visiting Asher twice in South Florida. Asher lived in a high-rise condo facing the Atlantic Ocean. The ninth-floor view from his windows was spectacular; it included the ocean and the Intracoastal Waterway, and it overlooked Birch Park. With a pair of binoculars, you could see the Miami skyline and multiple cruise ships departing from the Fort Lauderdale Port. On the beach, you could satisfy your curiosity by observing fishermen and sunbathers as well as men and women in bikinis and thongs.

Fort Lauderdale attracted movie stars, including Oprah Winfrey and David Cassidy; Dave Thomas, founder of Wendy's Restaurants, lived there too. The inventor of crayons and Lee Majors, the Six-Million-Dollar Man, resided in Broward County. The water taxi tour along the Intracoastal Waterway revealed to Mary and Asher just how desirable South Florida was to the rich and famous. Asher's real estate business would allow him to meet some famous persons.

Mary and Asher were visiting a nearby restaurant for brunch one day and ran into a famous comedian—Adam Sandler. Adam graciously said hello to Mary and smiled at her. Of course, Mary was tickled to have met him. She let all her friends know that Mr. Sandler was nice and approachable (and funny, too). Perhaps Adam reminded Mary of a young Donald, also a nice gentleman with a funny side to him.

Mary made two trips to Florida, and Asher made two trips to North Carolina during their seven-month courtship.

When Mary flew down the first time to meet Asher, she wore a white flower to help him identity her in the airport. Asher said he could identify her by the flower and by her natural beauty even at age 72.

On the last trip Asher made to North Carolina, in August of 2001, he purchased a 3200-square-foot brick home on the golf course in the mountains of Ashe County. Asher was a long-time golfer. As he once told Charles, "I have done a lot of deals on the golf course."

Mary was excited about the home purchase because she knew this home acquisition meant commitment; marriage followed.

Asher was a realistic optimist who dealt with life as it came and accepted what he could not change, including the loss of his first wife and his lack of children. His mindset enabled him to deal with life's difficulties while at the same time, treasuring every moment. He enjoyed travel and seeing unfamiliar places, especially times spent on cruises. He also enjoyed boating. Once, he came within fifty feet of a submarine off the coast of Florida.

ELOPEMENT/WEDDING

After that courtship of seven months, Mary and Asher married in Florida, with no friends present, just as they had planned, with no agenda. Mary's family would have found making the trip a challenge, so it was best that the wedding ceremony was private.

After the honeymoon and the couple's return to North Carolina, Mary's children would throw a party, a dance and dinner at the Elks Lodge. It was fun, but as always there was a mixed bag of surface talk, hidden negative feelings, and even some chaos. As will be shown later, the marriage to Asher provided Deborah and Danny an opportunity for their hidden agenda of greed.

THE TRIPS

For ten years each Christmas, Charles's family would visit Florida. In contrast, Danny and Deborah were absent from these Florida Christmases. Danny had been recently divorced, after twenty-three years of marriage. Deborah and her husband and three grown children were preoccupied with their own family and grandchildren. Deborah and Mary had to be satisfied with phone calls at this holiday time.

Nevertheless, Charles's family stayed close to Mary and honored her desire to be close, so each Christmas they packed a minivan and travelled the thirteen hours to South Florida. In 2011, when Abigail relayed the message to Danny that Mary wanted everyone to visit her on Christmas, the now-single man with grown children resorted to his common emotionally insecure tactics of saying "I have never been invited to South Florida".

Charles and Abigail and their three children enjoyed Florida and Mary looked forward to their company. The marriage to Asher was more friendship and business-like rather than a deep abiding love story. And because of this type of marriage, Charles and Abigail kept their distance from Asher allowing him to choose the degree of closeness.

What kind of marriage did Mary and Asher share? Mary enjoyed her marriage to Asher, but it was more of a friendship than the deep love she had experienced with Donald and then with William. With her family and friends mostly in North Carolina, she missed them, being thirteen driving hours away from them in Florida.

Mary kept a journal, discovered after her death. Here is an entry dated 21 May 2005: "A mother can only be as happy as her unhappiest child; a child is depressed and unhappy, and I am depressed and unhappy."

Perhaps she was thinking about her son Danny, because he was divorced and had many troubled relationships.

THE PH.D.

Charles continued to advance his knowledge in engineering by taking graduate-level courses at North Carolina Agricultural and Technical State University. In one course he enrolled in, on photonics, his professor took a keen interest in Charles because of the meticulous manner of Charles's home-work write-ups.

Mathematics for Charles was a subject he had loathed in high school, favoring physics or English. Charles would later recount, on the day of his Ph.D. ceremony, that he had come a long way from high school folly, where he studied "fumes," meaning perfumes and car fumes.

For the professor, a Chinese-born immigrant, mathemat-ics was "the art of science," and he knew advanced study of engineering demanded rigorous calculations. The theory was wave propagation, and Maxwell's equations were fundamen-tal in the fields of photonics and electromagnetism.

Electromagnetics (EM) is the study of electric and mag-netic fields; fields are a mathematical construct of vectors ... representing radio waves, for example. A vector has a mag-nitude and a direction. An electromagnetic field arises from electric charges and currents. An electric field is a force field that acts upon material bodies by virtue of their property of charge, just as a gravitational field is a force field that acts upon bodies by virtue of their property of mass. A magnetic field is a force field that acts upon charges in motion.

Electromagnetism is all around us. In simple terms, every time we turn a power switch on, every time we press a key on our computer keyboard, or every time we perform a similar action involving an everyday electrical device, EM comes into play. Charles from an early age was fascinated by EM fields originating from antennas and radios.

When the professor was impressed with Charles's diligent math write-ups, he called him into his office one day. Dr. Y. wore thick glasses on his round Asiatic face. His office was messy, with many papers on his desk revealing calculations concerning light waves and fiber-optics lab experiments.

Charles was unsure how to interact with Dr. Y., since the professor was of Asian descent and most of Charles's undergraduate and Master's degree professors were American-born. Nevertheless, Charles found Dr. Y.'s demeanor and attitude amusing; he decided to give the talks a chance, with the possibility of performing research with this long-time tenured professor, then almost 68 years old. It turned out that Charles would do all of the research.

Dr. Y. traced his education to a colleague of Albert Einstein. Einstein attended the Solvay Institute at Harvard in 1939; with him was Leon Brillouin, the discoverer of the electromagnetic phenomenon known as Brillouin scattering, a process where a light wave (a photonic wave) that passes through a medium (like an optical fiber) generates a different wave detectable as a radio wave or microwave.

Leon Brillouin was the academic advisor to Dr. Y.'s future professor. And Dr. Y. would be Charles's professor, making Charles a fourth-generation student of Brillouin scattering, a subject that as few as one hundred of the world's scientists and engineers would study.

Later, Dr. Y. would encourage Charles to research Brillouin scattering and its application to telecommunication devices. His dissertation would be on "slow-light" devices.

Dr. Y. liked to talk in his office about the fundamentals of engineering and physics. He told Charles: if you do not know the simplest theories well, how can you understand the complex phenomenon? These talks and the new relationship with Dr. Y. reminded Charles of two people: his father, Donald, and Albert Einstein.

Donald had taught Charles how to use a hammer, saw, and T-square, simple tools, but his father was persistent in the proper use of them on repairing his rental properties.

Similarly, Albert Einstein once said, "Everything should be made as simple as possible, but not simpler."

Both men had emphasized the fundamentals.

Similarly, Dr. Y. was a fundamentalist, not of religion but of the laws of physics. Dr. Y. believed the universe was full of order ... whether in the ocean waves or a leaf falling from a tall tree. To Dr. Y., a falling leaf was not only subject to the law of gravity, but moved back and forth in an oscillatory fashion much like the oscillations found on the atomic level of matter.

Dr. Y. had learned from many years of study and experimentation that the theories of electromagnetism, and thus light waves, could be resolved into only a few simple equations. For example, gravity and electromagnetic wave propagation would be unified into one or two governing equations. Moreover, all the research Dr. Y. had done, from his work as a graduate student to the many theses and dissertations he guided, would now culminate with Charles in a series of publications and a Ph.D. in 2010. But the road to get there would be long and narrow.

Dr. Y. was adamant that the "well" of research in Brillouin scattering was deep and dry—so dry that Charles would have to dig even deeper to find any new "nuggets." Charles used his hands-on skills in the laboratory to assemble and construct experiments involving lasers, fiber optics, and optical-to-electronic converters. For Charles, his goal was to discover something new about the wave shape of light signals as they passed through fiber optic threads, "light tubes" he called them. After a year of diligent research, Charles thought he had discovered a novel idea. He was wrong.

Once, Charles brought to Dr. Y. some experimental findings Charles thought significant, to which Dr. Y. responded harshly, "Your work is superficial. You need to dig deeper for something new and unique."

He pushed the lab results back to Charles, who left ever more determined.

Determination was a trait Charles learned from his father and, to a lesser extent, his wrestling coach in high school. Not shy about physical sports, Charles was somewhat smaller than most football players, but that did stop him from playing backyard football and flag football until his late twenties.

His high school wrestling coach would be instrumental in Charles's physical toughness and wrestling in college. But Charles did not like his college wrestling coach; after one season, he quit the team. Quitting the college team was a decision that would haunt Charles for more than two decades, until a reunion with his high school coach rekindled their friendship and provided closure to a once-disappointing outcome.

Dr. Y. was a mentor to Charles because they shared similar interests, despite coming from two opposite sides of the cultural and religious spectrum. Overcoming these differences, Charles's passion to respect and learn more about Dr. Y. forged a more than superficial relationship. Dr. Y.'s gentle yet demanding spirit motivated Charles to be a better student and person.

After completing his Ph.D., Charles wrote in his journal:

"In 2007-2010, I did research at NC A&T on the properties of light in optical fibers. The purpose was to 'control' telecom data packets for the Internet. So much for trying to 'control' something. There were experimental results obtained by our colleagues and other scientists our research could not explain.

"If one cannot explain chaos, one can choose the explanation from 'Divine sources.' Even the atheist colleague quoted *Genesis 1:3:* 'God said let there be light, and there was light.'

"Light came before the electron. How does one know there is a Supreme Power, the God of the universe? Look toward the 'light', not the darkness. You cannot hide light. One cannot hide the truth either. The truth sets one free—'light' sets one free. The *Bible* through cultural and tradition changes has survived time, and there is truth in the *Bible*. Therefore, John 3:19 says: 'This is the verdict: Light has come into the world, but people loved darkness instead of light because their deeds were evil.'"

THE DEED

Mary's relationship with her children had been faltering since she started dating Morris and even more so after marrying a millionaire, Asher. She spent half her time in Florida and half her time in the North Carolina mountains. She missed her families in North Carolina and Virginia deeply because she still carried Donald's dream with her everywhere she went; furthermore, the nice weather in Florida could not compensate for family time. This dilemma was only part of the story that changed in 2011.

Mary's devotion to family also meant she expected her children to come to see her often, but this was not always how things worked out. Asher was getting older, now almost ninety-four years old, with his vision deteriorating rapidly and his bodily functions also changing, causing Mary to care for a husband more than the typical spouse. She was somewhat like his nurse or his home health aide.

A lot of Asher's responsibilities, such as meals, health check-ups, and domestic duties, fell on Mary. She also had to drive him to appointments, prepare his meals, and take care of his personal affairs, while he sat and watched his stocks grow from $5 million to $8 million. His life was quite limited, mostly watching his fortune grow.

Asher was considered a wealthy man, but you would not know that by the habits of his spending. He wore jeans and T-shirts; on dinner dates, he paid for his and Mary's meals. Rather than having a giving spirit, it appeared this millionaire initially resented all the children and grandchildren Mary brought into the marriage. But as time grew, Asher's affection would too....

Deborah and Danny did not visit Mary in Florida; they resented the husband Danny called "the old man." However, Charles's young and thriving family looked forward to the thirteen-hour trip down I-95 to the sunny beaches of Florida. The family would stop in Savannah and visit the antique shops; this area was where the book *Midnight in The Garden of Good and Evil* was born.

Mary was always excited for Charles's family to visit Florida for the Christmas holidays. She looked forward to this time every year, a tradition she and Donald started when Charles was a young lad. Christmas for Donald had not been about presents; rather, he cherished carols and a warm, glowing fireplace and his friend Polly.

Charles and his family visited Florida from 2002 until 2014, when Mary's health limited her and Asher to remaining in North Carolina.

One evening, Charles and his family went out for dinner with Mary and Asher. When the meal check came to the table, Asher surprisingly decided to pay for only his meal, clearly leaving the remaining balance of $65 to Charles. Now, meal etiquette and the "art of manliness" is all part of chivalry. Charles decided not to complain about the meal cost, since in theory he was responsible for his own family. Still, this niggling lack of generosity rankled.

Some other concept of manliness, of masculine etiquette seemed appropriate. A useful and universal rule to remember is that the one doing the inviting, the one responsible for getting a dinner party together, usually should be the one to pay. If you have been invited to dinner, then you are the guest, and it's unlikely that you'll be responsible for picking up the bill. And if an event was arranged by mutual assent, then in all likelihood everyone will be going Dutch, sharing the expenses. Charles assumed Mary and Asher, his mother and stepfather, would pick up the dinner bill. It was not until later that he read about some subtleties concerning dining with in-laws.

While some of the guidelines for dining with your in-laws are the same as the universal rule, there are a couple of different scenarios to consider. For females, dining with the in-laws does not carry as much pressure when the check or bill arrives at the table. Abigail was present, and a daughter-in-law will never be expected to pick up the tab, or even deal with paying the bill, unless she happens to be dining with her in-laws without her significant other. (In that case, she should offer to pay her share — or theirs, too, if she's feeling generous — but she shouldn't be surprised or fight back too much if her in-laws insist on paying the whole bill.)

For the male dinner guest, when dining out with his wife's (or even girlfriend's) parents, it can be a little more awkward. In many scenarios, as with your own parents, the in-laws will just pay for the dinner, and it won't be a problem. But you should offer to pay your part.

The dinner guests of Asher and Mary knew they were financially secure. However, financially secure, the couple still had issues of time, health, energy, relationship as many elderlies have. Despite all these issues, Charles viewed Asher as a father-figure, although Charles accepted that Asher was not his father, nor had been William in many ways. Formally, however, each had been his stepfather, a position closer than being an in-law.

One of the issues brewing was: if Mary died, would Asher take over all of her estate?

Danny, who never presented himself and his family in Florida, loathed this possibility, once stating to Charles on the phone after the wedding, "If Asher takes all that my daddy worked for, I will kill him."

Charles thought to himself, why is Danny so against Asher? After all, Asher is a multi-millionaire, and the addition of a few hundred thousand dollars in his nineties would do little for adding to his wealth. Charles could not predict that Danny would one day take advantage of Asher and his estate. For that time, in 2011, Danny just resorted to complaints about Asher and to attempts to manipulate his mother to satisfy his false claims.

Charles remembered what his father Donald had said about Danny in 1979: "Danny will never listen. He always thinks he is right about everything."

In 1979, Charles admired his father's soft-spoken words, and by 2009, Danny's true character of narcissism was more evident than ever before.

Those who happen to live or work with a narcissist know

all too well how problematic such relationships can be. For a narcissist, almost everything is about him, despite his hidden agendas.

As Donald told Charles about Danny: "He can never be wrong."

It was not as though Danny was arrogant because he actually did "good deeds." With the comments toward Asher and Mary and with hiding from confrontation as well as slandering the couple, Danny was a "snake in the grass" in Charles's estimation.

Charles wondered if others really would find themselves agreeing with him and see the narcissism in Danny's self-serving, insensitive actions, even though masked by "good deeds." Understanding an egotistical individual's inner workings is no easy task.

The mountain house farm that was part of Donald's dream now legally belonged to Asher and Mary due to marriage—their names were on the deed. Mary was beginning to have concerns about who would inherit "Rainbow's End Lane" if she passed away. Donald's dream would not leave Mary's mind.

Mortality is a concept fifty-somethings start to think about, but Mary was busy with life and had not given it real consideration. After all, her middle-aged life was both traumatic and luxurious, being married to a millionaire and living in a high-rise condo overlooking the Atlantic Ocean.

By age eighty, however, the end of her life was something Mary was beginning to think about. Several other factors contributed to her concern about the mountain house, mostly the love-hate relationship with the controlling nature of Danny and the fact that part of Donald's dream was that the mountain home was for all the family, not just a few.

Danny was a hard worker, a trait he inherited from his parents. Donald and Mary were raised during the Depression, when jobs were few and putting food on the table was considered a blessing from God. For Danny, making money was not a blessing but a competition with his acquaintances, "keeping up with the Joneses," "win at all costs," as well as "only the strong survive."

Despite Danny's ability to make manual labor pay, he did not practice the ethics his father believed in, such as generally accepted accounting principles (GAAP). If, for example, there were no sales sticker on a piece of lumber he was buying at the hardware store, he would try to convince the clerk of a lower price, rather than wait for the clerk to confirm the store price or speak to a manager. Such unethical "little things" seemed insignificant to Danny, but one day Danny would be confronted about his bartering approach to business transactions, which irritated him. The irritation and hidden agendas are symptomatic of "cutting corners," an unethical business practice.

Nevertheless, Danny's core philosophy, and his strategy, was to convince his mother, Mary, that he would do all the chores and maintenance at the mountain farm and in return receive all of the property one day as his "God-given right." This discredited view goes back to feudal days and "primogeniture," the supposed rights of the first-born. The problem would be that no legal document existed to prove his claims. Moreover, Charles would attest one day that their father never intended for the mountain farm to be inherited by only one child of the patriarch.

In 2011, Mary changed the deed to her 40-acre mountain property, dividing equally this asset between her two sons, Danny and Charles. Mary kept a life estate option on the deed. Unfortunately, Mary did not communicate the change in an effective manner to each stakeholder.

Mary had pondered her decision to change the deed for most of 2011, seeking counsel from close friends, usually a worthwhile endeavor. Psychologists will tell you that most people have only enough emotional energy for one or two close confidants. In other words, most human beings do not have the time or energy to develop deep abiding relationships with more than two or three other beings.

Mary had two or three close friends and shared her need to change the deed with Billie. Billie and her husband were close friends with Donald during the time he was working on the mountain house until he passed away in 1988. Billie and her husband advised Mary to divide her assets equally among her three children and not worry about possible fallout from Danny.

Mary conveyed the news to Charles in person before returning to Florida in the fall of 2011. She handed him a copy of the deed which showed equal ownership between him and Danny. However, she was not effective in communicating the major change to Danny, mostly due to waiting too long to tell him.

Danny's birthday was in March of 2012. She enclosed the new deed in a birthday card and mailed it to him after she returned to Florida, six months after Charles knew about the new record. Charles did not tell Danny either, because this would have violated his mother's trust; she wanted to inform Danny her way.

Mary's method of communicating a legal document having strong emotional overtones, without any preface or discussion, demonstrated she was fearful of Danny's reaction. Rather than facing her fear head-on and "speaking the truth in love," she displayed reluctance, even cowardice. She did what so many do when faced with a controversial issue; she hid, because she did not want to deal with Danny's false belief that his father promised him the whole mountain farm, all forty acres and the house.

Here, a little history of Danny, his mother, brother Charles, and the mountain house is appropriate. After Mary married her third husband, Asher, in 2001, moving to live seven months per year in Florida, she proposed that property maintenance of the farm be divided proportionally between Danny and Charles. Danny, 12 years senior to Charles, was a "successful" owner of an auto body shop and agreed to pay for the cable TV and heating oil, while Charles, the engineer, would take responsibility for the electrical and phone bills. Both sons would share in the summer mowing of the three-acre field surrounding the house. Charles decided to take ownership of the landline telephone and electricity accounts while Danny arranged for periodic orders of heating oil.

In 2005, four years after Mary's marriage to Asher, Charles decided he should phone his brother Danny and try to get to the bottom of the mountain house responsibilities.

The phone conversation went something like this: "Danny this is Charles. I wanted to talk to you about the mountain house."

"Ok, what do you want to talk about?" asked Danny.

"Momma said she was going to leave the mountain house to both of us, so I think we should discuss the responsibilities."

Danny became defensive and said, "You have no idea what it costs to keep a second property up. I have spent countless weekends and my own money to keep this property going."

Danny's comments and attitude once again confirmed to Charles he was dealing with someone hard to get along with—just as Donald had told Charles about Danny when Charles was a little boy.

In a phone conversation in 2006, Danny told his mother he was planning to "build a barn" to store his mower and tractor. Mary continued to live in Florida most of the year; she approved of a "barn" being constructed, not realizing the true size of Danny's construction project. Mary was not frequenting the mountain home as much due to her marital responsibilities with Asher. She relied on Charles and Abigail to keep her informed of the status of the farm.

Mary had no idea the "barn" would be a two-car garage and an upstairs apartment (c. 1,000 sq. ft.). Danny utilized the help of some friends to construct the apartment and paid a day carpenter to frame and plumb the upstairs apartment. Although Charles was somewhat aware of the scope of the project, having assisted with some foundation work while visiting the farm in 2009, neither he nor his mother were ever consulted about the overall project—one that affected the farm's property value (c. $285,000) and tax obligations. Danny had no clue what it meant to manage and lead a project such that all stakeholders are aware of significant issues that would affect the overall outcome. As will be seen, this project undermined Donald's dream.

Divorced in 2005, Danny completed the garage apartment at an estimated cost of $65,000 and continued to maintain the overall property, spending his money on the property in greater proportion than Charles.

Mary told Charles privately the farm would be left to the two sons, while her daughter, Deborah, who had no serious interest in the farm, only wished to receive cash from her mother's future estate and would not share in the property in question. She would receive one-third of the cash value of the farm.

In 2009, Charles and Danny had a phone conversation about their mother's desire to change the deed. Both men did recognize and appreciate that her health was starting to decline, and she wanted to avoid the property's being inherited by her third husband.

The phone conversation with Danny began with mutual consent that the husband (stepfather) could inherit the property by law. The focus on this liability quickly turned to Danny's defending how expensive it would be for Charles to maintain the property and how much work Danny had already performed—Danny emphasized how much money he had invested in the property (namely the new "barn" and a new roof on the old frame house).

Charles told his wife, Abigail, how disappointing it was that Danny never consulted to him on the replacement of the old farm house roof in 2003. Danny never asked Charles to help or contribute to the roof project. When Mary tried to pay

Danny for the roof, he declined the offer. Finally, Danny stated during the phone conversation that he desired to own the property outright. Moreover, his tone and speech were intimidating because of his defensive tactics and selfish style and lack of a cooperative spirit.

When a person needs to communicate something vitally important to another person, face-to-face conversation is usually the method best suited to produce a win-win scenario or build trust. Although social media was not used to communicate the issue, a phone conversation is less effective than a face-to-face meeting; even the use of a mediator may be necessary.

Charles's impression was that Danny felt he deserved all of the property, based on his informal suggestion to acquire Charles's interest and ownership in an earlier 2001 face-to face conversation with Mary present. The conversation took place at the mountain house informally in the meadow, rather than at a previously scheduled formal meeting at a table, where everyone would know the agenda beforehand.

Charles disagreed with his brother's position that he deserved all of the mountain property and his claim that he did all the work. Charles's philosophy was based on a common principle of inheritance: the parent chooses how to divide her estate, not the child, not the heirs.

By 2012, Danny had significantly reduced his time visiting at the property since the deed transfer, stifling communication with Charles and to a lesser extent with Abigail, as well as avoiding family gatherings that would enable discussions of the deed transfer and its implications—something that worried Mary.

In her heart of hearts, Mary sought to reach an understanding between all parties for the property to be reclassified as a family place, part of Donald's dream. However, based on Danny's comments to Charles during their 2011 phone conversations, Danny asserted his sole ownership and proposed

Charles's relinquishment of the property by selling, or even giving up, the inheritance.

Charles and Danny agreed there was an issue with handling the farm's responsibilities, but they did not agree on the terms. Danny may have believed Charles's interests in the property were lacking or misaligned with his, but this was incorrect. Danny believed Charles could not afford to share responsibilities, that he did not have enough money to maintain the property; this later turned out to be false.

The conflict was not only over the mountain home and the dream Donald had. The conflict included multiple issues, starting with Mary's deed change, along with the purpose and use of the property, as well as its general maintenance. The deed transfer conferred equal ownership to Charles and Danny, aligning it with Donald's original intention that the farm be a family place, not a business nor under the control of one family member.

The issue at hand became how to cooperate on, enjoy, and maintain the property. For this goal to be met, Danny needed to have an understanding and agreement with Charles, with compromises for both parties to reach a win-win outcome—a family-centered win, not a person-centered loss.

The farm owners' original purpose was to have the farm be shared in both the amenities and chores proportional to family members' availability, and Danny's desire for sole ownership was inconsistent with this. The discussion on the phone in 2009 between Danny and Charles opened the door to reach some agreement on individual responsibilities and resources, but the farm's true purpose was not discussed. Future negotiations were a necessity, as Danny and Charles each owned the property evenly and thus needed to cooperate and define responsibilities.

DEBORAH

To Abigail and Charles, sister Deborah appeared to be following the moral code, but they would conclude she became "guilty by association" with Danny. Deborah's support of Danny's illicit power in the two estates and her association and approval of Danny's manipulative tactics with his mother as well as her lack of impartially regarding Charles and the mountain house made her guilty of abetting Danny's misbehavior.

DANNY

Danny was by all accounts a successful businessman, a law-abiding citizen, civic-minded, opinionated, controversial, said to be highly individualistic as well as opportunistic and "hard-working."

Danny was a father-like figure to Charles during the younger man's teen years. Although Donald was Charles's hero, Danny stepped in to help his mother take Charles to school or ball practice. Danny taught Charles how to work on cars, play baseball, and several other typically male skills. But Danny never had it in him to teach moral or ethical principles, ideals that Charles only touched briefly in his later life.

The relationship between Danny and Charles was superficial, characterized by verbal abuse and jealousy. Charles witnessed the verbal abuse between Danny and his ex-wife, an unhealthy, deprived relationship exhibiting pathological jealousy. Thus, Charles was implicitly taught to fear his older brother rather than love him or even like him. This was true of many Spencer family members and their eventual spouses.

Danny showed he could also be unethical and secretive, as demonstrated by not including his own mother in several improvement projects to the mountain farm. If you disagreed with him and did not praise him, he would avoid you and not include you in his farm property projects. On the surface, the Spencer family appeared to be in good working order, but troubled relationships were brewing, yet no one would talk about the situation.

What most family members did not see was Danny's obsession with impressing his mother. At the same time Danny told his mother Charles did not work around the mountain house and farm, complaining about Charles's lack of work at the farm during the time Mary was living in Florida. He complained about this during the time when he was building the garage-apartment for his own use.

Charles offered to help fund a new farm house roof, but Danny declined both to Charles and to his mother, claiming Charles had no time to help and complaining of his younger brother's prior lack of interest in the property.

On another occasion, Charles asked Danny if he planned to sell his sole ownership of their childhood home. Charles was interested in the home place and Danny responded: "You don't want that place."

Danny's management style and tactics were not conducive to win-win negotiations, as he had a "winner takes all" mentality—being a competitive pie slicer, not a pie enhancer and sharer. In Danny's mind, he was always right, with no consideration or empathy for the other person. He shied away from powerful men because he knew he could not control them.

Unfortunately, conflicts in family are typically not discussed openly; crucial differences in preferences or interests are downplayed, as was the case with Danny and Charles. Paradoxically, these differences should have been made to surface, to allow both men the opportunity to create value-added tradeoffs and development of contingency plans to grow the pie, not simply slice it up.

Up to this point, negotiations were abbreviated and based on a model of a "fixed sum." Danny's desire was to own the entire farm—as demonstrated by independently building the garage-apartment, offering to buy out Charles, making independent upgrades to the old frame house without consulting his mother (the legal land owner), and treating family members unpleasantly and without a spirit of cooperation.

To resolve conflicts over land issues, family members need

to arrive at a consensus, a mutual understanding among all the parties. In order for consensus to occur, the family members need to meet to resolve whatever their land issues are.

To expand the pie of preferences, interests, and resources with Danny, Charles would need courage and humility to seek an understanding of all the issues. The issues surrounding the conflict were emotional, as Danny made dramatic verbal statements (i.e., "nothing will come between me and my brother and sister") that contradicted his actions (becoming angry when Mary proactively changed the gate and door locks at the farm in 2012).

Consequently, tactful and empathetic management would be required to reach a win-win agreement. An effective pie-expanding strategy is to ask questions about the other party's interests and priorities, a strategy Charles did not practice in dealing with Danny.

One reason negotiations fail is when negotiators haggle over a single issue, for example, deciding who will pay the electrical bill. To unbundle all the issues in this farm feud would likely result in an integrative or win-win agreement. Since Danny's view of the mountain property was different from Charles's, rather than debating who had done the most work on the property, the focus should have been on a contingency contract where both parties obtain their interests, complementing the other, and appreciating each other's strengths.

An example of Danny's controlling behavior is illustrated in the bizarre relationship between Mary's third husband, Asher, and the eldest son's greed and manipulation of the elderly man.

Asher never had children of his own. He did not fully understand the desire a mother has to watch her children and grandchildren grow and mature. Mary's love for her children's development and success was captured in her journal, "No matter how old you are, you watch your children for improvement."

One day, after Asher and Mary returned to their mountain

condo from Florida, she decided to go to the grocery store. It was May of 2013, and her drive to the store would be interrupted. In the warmer weather, from May to October, Mary and Asher stayed in the mountains at a condo overlooking a golf course...about nine miles from the mountain farm. Their agreement was to live in Florida during the colder period from October until Mother's Day.

A poor country farmer driving an old, heavy-duty Cadillac ran a stop sign and slammed into Mary's Mercedes-Benz. The impact of the man's car was hard on the driver's side, but Mary's well-engineered car helped keep her injuries few. The air bag was a life-saver, but Mary suffered many bruises from the airbags.

Mary was taken by ambulance to the local hospital. The first person she called was Asher, but he did not answer the phone, because he was hard of hearing. Their neighbor witnessed the accident and upon return home, told Asher in person and then took him to the hospital to meet Mary.

Mary used her cell phone to call Deborah and Charles and lastly Abigail. She told Charles by phone: "Charles, I am okay, and I wanted you to know I was in a car accident, but I am okay."

She repeated this statement several times. When she told Abigail, Abigail wanted to know if Danny had been informed. Mary said no. Abigail asked Mary if she could call Danny to which Mary replied, "Do what you want."

Mary did not call Danny because they were estranged for the prior two years, estranged because the mountain farm deed was changed, infuriating Danny. Danny had stopped talking to his mother and gave her the cold shoulder

Abigail decided to call Danny. She told him about the accident.

His response was, "Who did the old man hit?"

Abigail said, "An old man hit your mother."

Danny never asked how his mother was or about any injury to the other party. He did ask where the car was, a response that focused on material possessions and not his own mother's well-being. Abigail told Danny she did know where the car was, and that his mother was in the hospital, to which Danny replied he would call her.

Danny sent his friend Mark to retrieve the car. He did not go immediately to see his mother. Finally, two days later, he came to the hospital.

The diagnosis of Mary's condition was high blood pressure and bruising to her chest and side from the air bag impact. She did not know then that she had multiple myeloma which two years later would take her life. Her dream, to see Donald's dream come true, would now be in jeopardy.

THE MIDDLE EAST TRIP

After five years of working full-time and acquiring his Ph.D. in 2010, Charles decided to go work for a long-time mentor, Lester. Lester was owner of a successful consulting and manufacturing firm three hours' drive from Charles's home. Despite job prospects in Upstate New York and other out-of-state cities, Charles weighed heavily the fact that Abigail enjoyed North Carolina, and Lester's firm was a safe opportunity. So, he accepted Lester's offer.

Among other leadership roles, Charles was responsible for some international projects in Mexico, Asia, and the Middle East. Charles loved to travel, and, unlike some business travel, Lester encouraged Charles to enjoy the culture after the work was done. One international project turned out to be unsuccessful for the firm but personally rewarding for Charles. The venture was to the country of Oman, situated near Saudi Arabia and Yemen.

Lester was a master at marketing, using social media to the fullest to capture new prospects. He would sit in his office all day and tally up the Google searches for his firm. Some of the new business did come from Google searches. One such hit was from an Internet technology (IT) firm in Muscat, the capital of Oman. The IT firm was hired by the government of Oman to analyze and fix a technical problem at the country's AM radio station near the United Arab Emirates (UAE) border and the Persian Gulf.

The contact at the IT firm was Ravi, an Indian-born, thirty-something man who knew English well but knew little about AM radio transmitting equipment. Lester's firm knew a lot about broadcast engineering, which would be needed to correct the problem with the antenna system situated in the desert of Oman, four hours from the nearest major city. The Oman government's AM station broadcast information to its citizens, who relied heavily on AM radio to obtain the news and weather.

The problem was that Iran was broadcasting on the same channel, the same frequency as Oman. The Iranian broadcast was full of propaganda that the Oman government did not want their people to hear. Why was Oman on the same frequency? Because of Iran's political power; Oman would not want to threaten them. Thus, the government relied on the IT firm and Charles to fix the technical problem.

Charles visited Oman twice, the first time to make electrical measurements on a six-inch-diameter transmission cable that connected two lattice towers. The cable carries the electrical signal from the transmitter that is then split among the towers and propagated to the Omani people hundreds of miles across country.

Ravi would not meet Charles at the Muscat Airport; rather, he sent a taxi driver escort to transport Charles to Ravi's office. Arriving in Muscat, Charles felt the warm air, could see the sand and the Arab people. In Oman, Islam is the state religion; both sexes tend to dress conservatively, with men generally wearing an ankle-length collarless gown, a "dishdashi," and women a long black dress called an "abaya."

Charles's European look and demeanor got the attention of all the taxi drivers waiting at the airport. Charles wasted no time finding his driver, who took him to the Hilton Hotel. Despite jet lag, Charles would meet Ravi for a quick summary of the plans for visiting the radio station in the desert near the UAE, the United Arab Emirates.

The driver and escort for Charles and Ravi was a large man dressed in a white collarless gown. His name was Abdullah. The drive to the radio station would be four hours, so Charles was curious where they would eat and what these guys were really like. Were they married? Was the media stereotype of Arab men "ruling their wives|" really true?

The trip to the desert radio station was uneventful except for a brief stop for a bread wrap snack. When Charles asked where he should put his lunch trash, Abdullah said to just throw it in the restaurant parking lot. The country was definitely not clean.

The other activity on the road to the radio station was a required border-guard check of the Jeep. The Jeep Charles was riding in had to cross part of the UAE to reach the remote Oman property. Charles realized other countries than the U.S. take their border patrol very seriously. Charles was anxious lest his test equipment be confiscated.

Finally arriving at the radio station, Charles was eager to get started with his work. Several Arab men were present at the station. While performing his work, Charles noticed the men would stop and drop to their knees in the desert and bow to worship Allah.

In Muslim etiquette, bowing is reserved for God. Islamic prayer consists of two types of bowing: *ruku* and *sujud*. *Ruku* is done during the *salat* —the obligatory daily prayers—and is done in a standing position with the back parallel to the ground. *Sujud*, also most commonly associated with the *salat*, is a full prostration. The person taking this posture places his forehead, nose, palms, knees, and feet on the ground.

The government of Oman does not keep official statistics on religious affiliation, but three quarters of Omanis adhere to the Ibadi sect of Islam, while the remaining twenty-five percent are either Sunni or Shia Muslims.

The measurements Charles took revealed impurities inside the cable. Charles was delighted his findings were rapid. The business contract only allowed for Charles to analyze the cable, not to fix it, as he would have to procure special parts.

He and Ravi quickly hit off a pleasant relationship. They decided to have dinner together after a long day in the desert. The town they would stay in was called Al Burami. The Al Burami Hotel was the only international hotel nearby. Charles walked in, saw a picture of the Sultan, and relied on Ravi to confirm the reservation. The hotel room was simple. The beds included no mattress. The beds were softwood. Charles could hear the loudspeaker's call-to-prayer the next morning.

He and Ravi enjoyed a traditional Arab meal before visiting the station one more time.

On Charles's second trip to Oman, he was required to carry more test instruments and parts to repair the faulty transmission line. Although the first trip, meeting Ravi and diagnosing the problem, had been a success, the second trip would prove to be challenging for Charles from a cultural and business standpoint. Charles attempted negotiations with the IT firm's president, who demanded Charles stay another week, exceeding the initial contract terms.

Charles departed the plane and entered security area of the Muscat Oman Airport. The security measures were obvious: policemen and bag screening. Charles was carrying a "Pelican" case, a hard, plastic briefcase inside of which was a radio frequency (RF) electrical impedance analyzer. The label on the case stated, "RF test instrument." The policeman questioned Charles at just about the time Charles was to carry it toward the exit door to meet Ravi.

Charles had reviewed the security measures, but he was traveling alone and could not speak Arabic, only the word

"Salaam," a word that literally means "peace," but is also used as a general greeting.

The Oman security measures required that all baggage (hand luggage and check-in baggage) of arriving passengers be subject to x-ray by Customs before exiting the airport. All electrical items such as laptops, mobile phones, cameras, mp3 players and entertainment devices might be subjected to additional screening.

"Please be prepared to remove your electrical items from the travel case to be x-rayed separately."

The policeman confiscated Charles baggage and demanded he come with him to the police station. Charles complied. Two days later, Charles had his test equipment and repair parts back in his possession.

During Charles's five-year work with Lester, he acquired some "soft skills" and sales tactics from this entrepreneur and mentor, the seventy-year-old owner of a consulting firm in eastern North Carolina. From 2010 to 2015, Charles worked for Lester on various engineering and sales projects, often traveling the world to meet clients, including some from the countries of Oman and Mexico.

DETAINED IN RUSSIA

Prior to joining Lester's firm, Charles completed his Ph.D. The last publication related to his dissertation was on the characteristic of light pulses in optical fibers. Something strange and peculiar happens when light is sent down from a laser through a small (nine micrometer) optical fiber at a specific intensity. These are the same fibers that connect millions of Internet connections today. An acoustic (sound) wave is created inside the fiber such that an electronic signal can be detected on an oscilloscope. Charles submitted his paper to the Moscow Conference on Photonics in the spring of 2010. The conference would commence in August 2010, the same week as Lester's hiring of Charles. Charles asked Lester if he could delay the start date to allow visiting Moscow.

Not only would Charles visit Moscow, but he contacted a Russian engineer who would provide a tour of a high-power shortwave broadcasting facility. Charles planned to write a blog for Lester on the trip to the transmitting facility. The other arrangements for the Moscow conference were assisted by a Russian lady who helped Charles obtain the invitation letter.

Charles received his invitation from Moscow University for the photonics conference, and since he had been traveling the world for some time now, his passport was up to date. Charles was excited about the trip and had researched places to visit in Moscow. His travel experience in Japan a few years back had convinced him the only way to really experience the culture of a new country was to meet the local folks and take a tour of key buildings, museums, and institutions.

Charles' Ph.D. advisor was a Russian-to-English translator. Dr. Y was excited for Charles to attend the Moscow conference.

Charles downloaded his American Airlines ticket, which showed a departure from Raleigh-Durham Airport to New York City's LaGuardia, then to Helsinki, Finland, and then St. Petersburg, Russia. Charles checked his baggage and showed all his paperwork to the gate agent in Raleigh.

The trip to New York was uneventful, a tight economy seat. Charles thought to himself *folks think traveling is all fun, but the economy seating is actually cramped and given security measures, airlines travel is not what is used to be in the 1970s or 1980s.* But Charles knew after the tragedies of 9/11, airline safety was more important than comfort.

In New York City, Charles checked in with the international flight agent who took a close look at his tickets and personal identification; Charles also showed his invitation to Moscow University.

Charles was pleased to learn he would be traveling in business class on an Airbus A330 which had reclining seats that folded out like a single bed. The audio/video service would be a plus, but Charles was tired, so he slept most of the way to Helsinki, waking up for two meals, breakfast and lunch. Helsinki was seven hours later in time than New York.

Arriving in Helsinki, Charles was pleased that all gates were located in one terminal building, along the same short walkway. He was then confident that he would reach his connecting flight quickly and hassle-free. The airlines on Charles's itinerary included Finnish Air, known for safety and excellent customer service. Charles would complain to himself at the fact many U.S.-based airlines customer service can be lacking, but the European hosts and hostesses of Finnish Air were marvelous. Finnish Air was reputed to be all things Finnish— clean, efficient, with fabulous service and excellent value. The airline prided itself on its service, and it showed in all areas; the food, the gift bag, and the in-flight entertainment.

The 45-minute trip from Helsinki to St. Petersburg was worrisome for Charles. He had communicated with the Moscow University assistant but had not checked his email in a few days, and something seemed to be missing in Charles's paperwork. But the excitement to see Russia had been building up in Charles for several weeks, overshadowing anything Charles may have left at home.

All Charles could think about was what Ronald Reagan had said in Berlin in 1987: "Mr. Gorbachev, tear down this wall."

The Russian Imperial Guard, officially known as the Leib Guard, were military units serving as personal guards of the Emperor of Russia. Peter the Great founded the first such units following the Prussian practice in the 1690s, to replace the politically motivated Streltsy. Charles wondered what type of security would be in place as he entered into Russia in the St. Petersburg Airport. Would there be guards that looked like the Imperial Army?

Charles had done his research on border security at Russia. At the passport desk, a Border Control officer would ask to see the passport or travel document and any supporting documentation necessary. Charles had his passport and letter of invitation from Moscow University. What Charles did not realize, after twenty hours of travel and airline security inspections in New York and Helsinki, was that he did not have one important thing, an important thing that would both help and hurt Charles on this trip to Russia.

Russian Air is not known for safety, but its cheap flight to Moscow from St. Petersburg was convenient for meeting the tight schedule to meet the engineer and write the story for Lester.

Charles checked his email in the St. Petersburg Airport. The female assistant had sent Charles an email asking him to confirm their meeting at the University in three hours. Charles was unaware that her invite was for him and some of the University students and professors who wanted to meet Charles at a private party in downtown Moscow. She agreed to arrange a taxi to meet Charles at the Moscow airport after a one-hour flight from St. Petersburg. Charles agreed to meet her there in three hours.

Charles also knew he was dealing with foreigners and a woman he never met before. Something in the back of his mind told him "hedges." The female assistant had sent more than a few emails, and the tone of the emails was somewhat provocative. So "hedges" kept coming back to mind ... and Abigail and their 20-year marriage.

With the divorce rate steadily climbing and infidelity creeping into even the happiest marriages, in a society that trivializes adultery and its devastating effects, with temptation and opportunity coming from all directions, Charles knew he better be careful; he re-read the email and noticed the email address was different and she signed the letter as "Waiting for you, Natalya." She even included a photo of herself, wearing a sexy dress and shown dining alone, a beautiful blonde, at a fancy hotel.

Charles was now alarmed. Was Natalya the University Assistant that sent the invitation letter for presentation of the Ph.D. paper or was she a prostitute?

Charles was an adventurous man, learning street smarts from several world trips and hanging out with many different type of folks from all levels of society in his prior 30 years.

Exiting the plane, Charles walked the Russian tarmac to the security area, up a ramp where the border guards holding what looked to be AK-47 rifles in their hands. Behind them was "the wall." The guards' facial expressions were blank and all business.

Still, Charles kept thinking about Ronald Reagan: "Tear down this wall!" the speech made by Reagan in West Berlin on 1987, calling for the leader of the Soviet Union, Mikhail Gorbachev, to open up the barrier which had divided West and East Berlin since 1961.

Charles felt uncomfortable as the men stared at him. *I look European, so what is the big deal with these looks?* Charles asked himself.

Charles arrived at the wall and a window with bars. On one side stood the guard and inside the window was another man who asked for Charles paperwork. "Your passport?" requested the guard. Charles presented his passport and also showed him the letter of invitation from Moscow University.

Charles's emotions were feelings of disappointment: he had failed to acquire a Russian visa. Had Natalya tricked him into the conference invitation? The document had been sealed and looked real.

Charles was embarrassed that his professional career might be affected by a stupid error in travel documentation. What would he tell Dr. Y. and Lester? Would he tell Abigail that it appeared he had cooperated with a prostitute and not a University official? The application fee of $300 possibly would be going to pay for prostitution services.

Charles pleaded for entrance into Russia, but the guards who now escorted Charles to the police station would accept no excuses. The guards appeared to question Charles on his purpose for going to Russia and detained him for 30 minutes.

Thankfully, a flight attendant on Russian Air saw the problem Charles was having and tried to assist in the negotiations. But you cannot negotiate with border patrol agents in Russia. The flight attendant must have felt empathy for Charles because he allowed Charles back on the plane, which would return to Helsinki immediately.

The last words Charles heard on Russian soil were from the border guard in the police station: "Go back!"

Charles felt dejected in the ride back to Helsinki as he sat in a rear seat in the old Russian plane. Where would he stay? Would the Finns understand him?

Upon arrival in Helsinki, Charles emailed Abigail, Mary, Danny, and Deborah. It was an attempt by Charles to receive empathy during a difficult day. That day would be even more difficult: Charles discovered his cell phone was not working. However, by asking one airline representative, Charles learned the musical giant Bono was playing in Helsinki that night, and hotels would be difficult to find.

Charles found a computer terminal in the airport and searched for hotels. The only hotel available was some 50 miles from the airport. Charles had exchanged dollars for Russian currency, now he had to find some Finnish money to purchase a taxi ride to the hotel.

The taxi drove Charles about one hour to a remote cottage-style place, and the dejected Charles would overcome jet lag the next half day sleeping somewhere so foreign to him, a place where cattle and sheep grazed the green pastures and tall skinny hardwoods stood like thousands of pencils balanced on their erasers.

Charles woke up, but it was near nightfall in Finland. He decided to take walk along wooden pathways on a journey through fields and forests, a relaxing way to reflect on all that had transpired the previous 30 hours. No phone and no food. He thought of Donald in the Hurtgen Forest of World War II and Donald's dream.

The walk would be cold, but the starry night would always be remembered. Optics and light was a new-found field of study by Charles; he took solace in the light.

For this night, the lights would come out in a spectacular show called the Northern Lights. In Finland, nature's most spectacular light show, the Aurora Borealis, becomes visible on roughly 200 nights a year.

Were these lights a "sign" Charles should accept as Divine intervention that the Russian trip was not meant to be. If Charles had entered Russia, the prostitution ring would surround him, perhaps risking his life as he knew it. This would not be the only risk to turn into a crisis, as will be seen shortly.

Charles spent the weekend in Finland. A visit to the Russian embassy did not provide an alternate solution to the failed attempt to enter Russia. Charles visited a few museums and churches before taking a flight back to New York City two days later.

When Abigail picked him up at the airport, he hesitated to tell the whole story. Honesty is a quality Charles's father embodied, but for some strange reason Charles was fearful the whole truth and nothing but the truth would hurt Abigail. Why not be totally honest about the Russian detainment and the apparent prostitute?

Charles was as guilty as Danny hiding the true self, instead attempting to mask hidden agendas. Danny was hiding his desire to take over his mother's estate, and Charles was hiding the fact that the Russian contact was actually a prostitute in disguise. Thankfully, Charles did not sleep with her.

BACK HOME

Charles continued to work for Lester, engaging in some interesting international projects but spending less and less time with Abigail and his children. The paycheck from Lester was steady and more than enough to keep all the bills paid and have a surplus to invest in college and financial retirement funds including AT&T stock. By 2013, Charles had amassed over 4,000 shares of AT&T stock, which was paying a fine 5.5 percent quarterly dividend. Dividends were something Charles liked to discuss with Asher, who would give advice on the younger man's company interests and personal stock account.

Charles and Asher slowly developed a father-and-son-like relationship after Asher and Mary were married in 2001. Charles knew Asher was reserved, and Charles would do nothing to disrespect the wealthy 96-year-old real-estate tycoon. Meanwhile, Danny had nothing to do with Asher except to utter slanderous or childish comments. For example, Danny ridiculed the old man for staying in his room all the time and for his daily alcoholic drink routine.

Charles soon realized Danny's negative comments about Asher were due to Danny's unhealthy self-image and insecurity. Charles surmised that folks with poor self-images often like to victimize others in an attempt to elevate themselves over the other more secure individual.

Danny believed he was a victim of being cheated out of full ownership of the mountain property and to a lesser extent, he resented a failed marriage he claimed was not his fault.

When Danny told Charles he was getting a divorce, Charles appreciated that for once Danny confided in a deep conversation, rather than some superficial "red-neck talk" too common with Danny.

But Charles would learn later, as will be explained, Danny was not purely a victim of divorce, because successful marriages are built on not just trust but commitment, passion, and intimacy ... elements Danny's marriage came to lack.

No partner is perfect and even if one partner commits the "grave sin," or breaks the moral code, the Judeo-Christian principle of marriage is "to death do us part," and the other partner can choose to forgive and reconcile. It's easier said than done.

Forgiveness is something that only needs one person. Reconciliation takes two. Charles would later learn this first-hand in his own marriage.

Meanwhile during the week, Charles traveled and worked on projects for Lester.

Lester and Charles visited Chamber of Commerce events. Both men and women attended these. Lester liked to mingle, touting his business, while Charles enjoyed the conversation, since his weeks were usually alone, without family.

CHAPTER 10

THE CAREGIVER FOR ASHER

A CAREGIVER FOR MARY

In April of 2015, as Mary's multiple myeloma got progressively worse, and the 97-year-old Asher could no longer help her, they agreed to hire a private nurse.

The interviews took place in private, with Mary and Deborah present. "We don't need to invite Charles – he's too busy and so is Abigail", Danny told Deborah in a private phone conversation.

But Abigail was concerned about Mary for many years prior to Mary's failing health while Deborah and Danny stayed at home during the Christmas get-togethers in Florida. Abigail would visit regularly, and she was present for the candidate Patty. Danny would be informed by Deborah who the candidates were, and if they were a fit for their schedules and management style. They wanted to be able to control the nurse, as opposed to having a nurse providing leadership and expert care.

Danny was a narcissist; this meant he wanted to control the nurse. Although his demeanor suggested sincerity, down deep, he wanted control over his mother and her elderly and ill husband Asher. A pawn for Deborah and Danny, the caregiver was likely a tool to manipulate Mary and Asher and keep information from Charles and Abigail.

Despite Charles and Abigail's eleven-year relationship with Asher, it appears Deborah and Danny did not want Charles and Abigail to have any more control in decision making concerning Mary or Asher.

Living three hours away, Deborah used text messages and some phone conversations to appeal to the emotions of Danny without researching the facts about the underlying family conflict. As the oldest sibling, she was weak-minded and held a bias against Charles without knowing the truth about Danny or her mother's affairs. So, when time came to choose a caregiver, Charles and Abigail, who had spent much more time with the elderly couple, were not consulted.

Charles and Abigail were close to Mary and Asher, visiting the elderly couple at their Florida condo and mountain condo on the golf course often since their wedding in 2001. By all accounts, there was much joy shared by Mary and Abigail, so much so that Deborah resented Abigail, much as Danny was jealous of Charles.

The caregiver chosen was Patty, not an RN, Registered Nurse, but an LPN, a Licensed Practical Nurse, somewhat less expert. She was a "sitter," a forty-something country girl with a smile who was never too shy to talk about the rumor of the day. She was very likeable and had some medical knowledge.

Except for Mary and Deborah, other nearby family members were not consulted about the hiring of Patty. Asher was not included in the hiring of Patty or informed of the plan, since they decided Mary would pay for her caregiver. Comments made by Deborah implied that Asher did not show enough concern for her mother's declining health. However, this was not true; Asher had his own health problems and could not care for his wife.

Deborah had her mother's health power-of-attorney because Deborah was a trained nurse. Mary felt she was qualified, and she desired to be close to her daughter. Deborah was living in Virginia, three hours away, while Abigail and Charles lived virtually down the street.

Mary and Deborah did not have a deep relationship, yet Mary thought the power-of-attorney assignment was the right thing to do, partly because Deborah was trained as a nurse. Mary wanted to be close to her family, but the health care power-of-attorney only enhanced their relationship ever so slightly. Their relationship remained shallow, as Deborah hesitated to share information that would strengthen their ties.

A Health Care Power of Attorney (HCPOA) is a legal document that allows an individual to designate another person to make medical decisions for him or her when he or she cannot make decisions for himself or herself.

The HCPOA designates someone who tells the doctors what to do or what not do for you. A person need not be terminally ill, elderly, or facing high-risk activities to execute a HCPOA. Health care decisions include the power to consent, refuse consent, or withdraw consent to any type of medical care, treatment, service, or procedure. A HCPOA is also sometimes referred to as a "health care proxy," "medical power of attorney" and/or "Durable Power of Attorney for Health Care."

Deborah and Mary discussed a plan and schedule with Patty. Asher, Charles, and Abigail were not included. The plan was to start out half-a-day, 8 a.m. to noon, and with doctor's appointments and any health care Mary would need. The nurse was not hired to help Asher. Asher did not want help at the time.

If Mary's multiple myeloma condition worsened, more hours would be added to Patty's responsibility. Patty came with high recommendations, having cared for one of Mary's friends who died from multiple sclerosis.

Prior to the hiring of Patty, Mary's condition had worsened. She knew she could not return to Florida, which disappointed

Asher greatly. Florida was where Asher wanted to die.

The caregiver, Patty, showed up during the middle of the day to attend to Mary's physical needs or household chores, including verifying medicine, preparing breakfast and lunch as well as cleaning up and talking to Mary. Any doctor appointments and medicine orders were handled by Patty.

Patty was responsible and professional while Mary was alive; however, after Mary's death, Patty's communication with Abigail and Charles stopped. She communicated only with Deborah and Danny, who in turn did not share information. The deep relationship Abigail and Charles forged with Mary and Asher over the past eleven years was now changed due to secrecy created by Deborah and Danny and to a lesser extent Patty.

Asher asked Charles and Abigail to return to Florida and retrieve some personal belongings, including precious items from his safe. The safe would be a pivotal item in the executor job as Asher became very ill. Asher trusted Charles to do this for him, and Charles honored his request.

Asher also trusted Charles with his mother's wedding ring and his father's wedding band. Charles would open the safe and discover hidden treasures about Asher and his earlier life: Marilyn Monroe stamps, old coins and pictures of his very attractive prior wife, Dorothy.

On Patty's first day of work, she came in while Mary was still asleep. Asher was not pleased to have Patty present. He did not know Patty because no one had included him on the original decision-making process.

Asher did not eat his breakfast, and angry about being left out of the decision-making, he verbalized his emotions by saying harsh words to Mary. Mary cried and then immediately called Abigail.

Abigail received the phone call from Mary while she was with her daughter, April, at the eye doctor. Abigail did not answer, but Mary left a voice mail. Mary was crying and said, "Abigail, I need you to come over."

After Abigail listened to the message carefully, she called Deborah to see what was wrong with Mary and the new caregiver Patty. Deborah told Abigail the reason Mary was upset was due to Asher's needing time to accept Patty.

Deborah's response was conflict avoidance: to let Mary and Asher work it out on their own. This is an example of cowardly behavior on the part of Deborah who was avoiding the conflict despite having the power to intervene.

Part of leadership inherently implies the leader includes his or her team members in the process. Anyone can be a manager of affairs, but not all managers are leaders. Clearly, Deborah and Mary wanted to manage Patty, but they did not practice effective leadership. Part of the reason they did not include Asher in the decision-making process was they did not think he really cared for Mary. As Deborah exclaimed "All Asher cares about is the stock market. He can't even give Mom a glass of water."

Mary wanted Abigail to come over to her home. They had a deep relationship forged because of Abigail's devotion to family, something she learned as a teen in a seven-person home.

Abigail went to see Mary. They talked in private in Mary's bedroom. Mary asked Abigail to talk to Asher. Abigail had a way with older individuals she had learned from her internship at a geriatric hospital. Abigail and Charles got along with older people well.

Abigail talked to Asher. Asher told Abigail that Patty was a stranger, and he did not want her in his home. He stated, "I live here too."

Abigail explained that Mary needed the help. Asher said he felt angry toward Mary and to a lesser degree toward Deborah. After explanation of the need for Patty, Abigail encouraged Asher to give this caregiver a chance.

Asher accepted the caregiver; it took a couple of months for him to get used to her. By this time, Mary's multiple myeloma had advanced to other ailments. She could no longer drive and needed to use a walker. She needed to drink lots of water due to bladder infections. She developed a *Clostridium difficile* infection, and it appeared that she needed a more highly-trained nurse, an RN, to take care of her.

Asher had a hearing impairment, so Deborah did not take the time to explain things to him. Instead, Deborah and Danny made fun of Asher. Deborah would call Danny, who lived a few miles away, and tell him about the events of the day. Deborah would tell Danny what Mary did and complain about Asher.

Although Deborah and Danny kept the caregiving issues to themselves, they failed to tell Abigail, the original caregiver, what was going on. They hid information that could have helped care for Mary and reduced confusion, rather than be team players and share information.

Danny made fun of Asher because he stayed in his room all day, monitoring his $8 million stock portfolio.

Elder abuse happens when a caregiver takes advantage of, or targets, the elderly, sick, and disabled. A caregiver, loosely defined, is anyone who cares for a person who cannot care for him or herself. The caregiver assists the patient or dependent with activities in daily life.

Thus, caregiver fraud can take the form of causing physical harm, endangering of health or body, theft, embezzlement, forgery, fraud, and identity theft, among other misconduct. Caregiver fraud can be committed by paid or unpaid caregivers, and by both licensed caregivers and individuals who deceptively claim to be caregivers. Recent instances of caregiver fraud in California and across the nation have ranged from fraudulent individuals stealing credit cards to posing as medical practitioners and charging exorbitant fees for services never provided.

This steep increase in caregiver fraud should incite elders, families, and advocates to be on guard and aware of the realities of caregiver fraud.

MARY'S LAST DAYS

During the last week of Mary's life, Deborah and Danny did not share information about their mother's funeral and the coordination of caregiving efforts concerning Asher.

Nevertheless, Charles remained quiet and steadfast respecting his mother. Charles wrote this poem right after Mary died. It is a tribute to her life, especially near the end, when she had so much pain:

A tribute is written
Not on account of the death of Mary
Who now rests in peace,
But for the more noble and glorious purpose of inspiring
    our youth
And captivating our mortality.

For we are all traveling
On the level of time
To that undiscovered celestial place
From whose bourne no traveler returns.

Death hath no sting to the traveler,
But the bystander forgets
Not Mary's hugs, kisses, or her timely aid and assistance
And yes, her family warmth
Her splendid meals
And the Almond Joy
We shared up to the end
And her favorite philosophy of "y'all sit and talk much."

If death has no sting,
Surely the Grand Deity
In all His glory and wisdom
Shines upon you and me today.
For this traveler did her duties,

Sacrificed much for her loved ones
And paid the price over and over
As wife three times,
Mother times three
Grandmother times eight, and
Great-grandmother times six.

Then she showed us
Who she really was as a fighter of pain
And the terrible cancer, multiple myeloma.

O, God, why do you allow cancer to give so much pain?
But she knew the Almighty
Despite the pain.

Pain was on the mind of the former atheist, C.S. Lewis, who turned to God and said to his countrymen:

Is it you that allow abuse and starvation and pain to your fellow man?
If you do, is it to know Almighty God better?
Why do you hurt others with your words?
Do you really know the Grand Creator and Supreme Architect?

C.S. Lewis also said, "The problem is not why some pious, humble, believing people suffer, but why some do not." [Extract by CS Lewis © copyright CS Lewis Pte Ltd.]

President William McKinley, the third American president to be assassinated, lived for several days after he was shot, and towards the end, his wife started crying and screaming, "I want to go too! I want to go too!"

The President's wife exclaimed this, and with his last measure of strength, McKinley turned to her and spoke his last words: "We are all going."

In pain it is the peace that passes all understanding which resides in Ms. Mary Lou.

> Rest in peace, dear soul,
> Blessed mother and honorable wife.
> Carry on, dear souls,
> Not with the purposeful duty and happiness
> That can come with this world
> But the travelers' legacy of love
> And sacrifice will reach that undiscovered country
> From whose bourne no one returns.

AFTER MARY'S DEATH

After Mary died, Asher was sad, and like many surviving spouses who are old, he became weaker physically. He needed more help with his personal affairs, and Abigail was always attentive to his needs the last twelve years.

The week after Mary's death, Deborah stayed in the bedroom next to Asher's office. While Abigail worked, Deborah hung around to help Asher, as well as to learn about the man she had no genuine interest in only six months prior.

Deborah spent her time talking to Patty and checking Facebook. Social media had become the main form of entertainment for many in Charles's extended family. Although Charles would use it to share photos with Mary, he doubted genuine relationships were strengthened through social media.

Deborah also made friends with the nursing home administrator who provided Deborah with the emergency contact form for Asher. Asher wanted Abigail and Deborah to be on the emergency contact form.

During the week that Deborah and her family were present,

when Mary had just passed away, Abigail saw the emergency contact form on the refrigerator had been tampered with and that her name was removed from the emergency contact list.

Abigail had been raised to tell the truth, and her missing name bothered her. She confronted Deborah. Since Deborah was the oldest sibling and had been present with Asher and Patty for over a week, it was natural for Abigail to ask Deborah about the name change. Deborah's reply was that she knew nothing about it, which was odd, but Deborah's non-verbal clues suggested she was either hiding something or was afraid to tell the truth.

Telling the truth, Charles would learn, was a moral principle he and his siblings failed to adhere to in several occasions. Deborah would rationalize what she had done, maintaining that hiding information about Asher and the emergency contact form was good for others, or to protect others, when in fact there was no mutual benefit.

So, Abigail, the faithful daughter-in-law of eleven years, confronted Asher about where her name was.

Asher replied, "I think Patty changed the name."

Asher stated to Abigail he wanted her to be his contact. Meanwhile, Danny tried to convince Asher that Abigail was not fit for the job, as she had a child at home, and not to bother her, while he would do her job.

This seemed to be evidence from Asher's comments, that Patty was a pawn for Deborah and Danny to play the game of manipulating Asher. After all, Danny had snooped around Asher's office and determined his stock portfolio was massive.

The thought of controlling Asher thrilled Danny.

My mamma will get some of that, somehow, some way, Danny thought selfishly. But Mary had just died, and the $2 million she was to receive to be inherited by her children could never be Danny's, legally anyway.

Danny did not always operate according to strict legal

practices, being a man who operated on his own terms at the emotional expense to others, a true narcissist with narcissistic personality disorder (NPD), a disorder with a long-term pattern of abnormal behavior characterized by exaggerated feelings of self-importance, an excessive need for admiration, and a lack of understanding of others' feelings.

After the mountain house deed and ownership were changed by Mary to include Abigail, Danny did what most narcissists do when they don't get their way: they go and hide and pout. Danny was a true control freak.

Why does someone become a control freak?

Our genes may account for many of our personality traits, and children copy the behavior they witness. If your parents were obsessive, domineering, or aggressive, then you are more likely to be that way too. But Donald was not a narcissist, and Danny and his mother shared some of the same traits. The difference was that Mary lived by the moral code, carrying on Donald's dream and their shared belief in God.

Jealousy and narcissistic tendencies stem from feelings of insecurity. This can result from losses experienced in childhood, including dying parents, divorced parents, or parents' being emotionally unavailable because of illness. Alcohol and cocaine can fuel jealousy and paranoia. Childhood trauma, abuse, or neglect can make it difficult for someone to trust others. Almost everyone knew Danny was jealous of Charles.

CHAPTER 11

THE STOLEN EXECUTOR JOB

In the summer of 2015, as Mary was becoming sicker with multiple myeloma, Deborah and her family came to visit Mary. It was customary for Mary to have all her children over for dinner. Charles and Abigail came over, and everyone gathered around the den to watch television.

Danny was not present, as he and his mother were not on good terms, due to the fundamental issue of the mountain deed change a few years back and Danny's negative feelings toward Asher and Charles.

Asher was tending to his business affairs in the adjacent office. Deborah's husband, Abigail, Charles, and Mary were carrying on some small talk in the den while the TV was on.

Then Asher came into the den and said, "Charles, can I talk to you for a moment?" "Sure, Asher. How can I help you?" exclaimed Charles.

Charles met Asher in the kitchen and just listened. Charles' past 10 years helping the 98-year-old multi-millionaire with his computer and discussing stocks had become special and routine so he was surprised by a serious question.

"Your mom is sick, and my nephew is not aware of some of the things going on, so would you be willing to be the executor of my estate if something happens to Mary?"

Charles replied, "Sure. I would be honored to be the executor."

"It will not happen without pay," Asher exclaimed.

This request to be a part of managing Asher's affairs was pleasing to Charles: it meant Asher trusted him, a father-figure handing over the reins to a son.

Asher also asked Charles to find him a local lawyer to rewrite his will. Charles then asked Mr. H. to be the lawyer; he came highly recommended and lived in the same retirement home as did Asher and Mary. Mary wanted to use Jacky, but Charles knew Jacky was a friend of Danny and was another controversial man, a man by all accounts was not above reproach.

Charles spent several hours arranging for Mr. H. to meet with Asher.

The executor of an estate is generally a person the deceased has named in his will, a person who submits the will to probate and then obtains control of the deceased's affairs by qualifying as his personal representative. The executor has a fiduciary duty — a duty of trust and integrity — to the estate's beneficiaries. While most people try to appoint trustworthy individuals as their executors, the case sometimes arises where a dishonest executor needs to be removed.

In August of 2015, Charles called the law office of Mr. H. and spoke to the assistant, Ray, who stated by voice mail that Jacky was handling the estate, not Mr. H. "Very strange", Charles pondered to himself.

Charles wondered why, since he was the executor, the attorney or Asher had not informed him of the attorney change. After the phone call, Charles told his wife Abigail, "I bet Danny and Jacky are scheming again." "I don't trust those men, you better get your own lawyer", Abigail pleaded with Charles.

In January of 2016, Asher had a minor falling accident. In previous wills up until February 2016, Asher always had a co-executor or back-up. But in February 2016 Asher's will was altered so that Charles was no longer the executor and with no back-up.

Most elderly folk do not change their will when they are about to die and are weak physically and mentally. For the prior will of Asher, Mary was the executor and Charles was the back-up. Then Asher changed the executor to Charles and wrote his nephew Chuck about the alteration.

Asher wrote: "Dear Chuck: My wife Mary is ill with cancer and you are not aware of some of the things happening in my life right now. I am adding Charles Spencer, Mary's devoted son to be the executor of my estate."

Asher is also recorded on tape as saying that Charles was the executor. According to North Carolina law, for an in-person conversation, the consent of at least one party to a conversation is required to record an "oral communication," defined as "any oral communication uttered by a person exhibiting an expectation that such communication is not subject to interception under circumstances justifying such expectation, but the term does not include any electronic communication." Thus, a person does not need consent to record conversations in public where there is no reasonable expectation of privacy.

Since Mary died in October, Charles and Abigail were unsure who then had power of attorney, and there were questions regarding the health power of attorney (proxy) change.

In November of 2015, Charles wrote Asher a letter which read:

Dear Asher,

Last week you asked me, Charles Spencer, to be the power of attorney for your estate. Do I need to contact your attorney Mr. H. and have him call you regarding the power of attorney change?

Sincerely,
Charles

Also in November of 2015, Charles called Mr. H.'s office and spoke to the firm's paralegal, Ray. Ray told Charles that he was still the executor and held the power of attorney.

"Your name is all over the will and estate papers; I don't think you have anything to worry about.... Charles, you are the executor, with power of attorney and health power of attorney," stated Ray by telephone.

After Mary's death, Danny showed up at Asher's home each morning to bring over breakfast and talk secretly with caregiver Patty. "If Asher needs anything, you call me, Patty—not Charles or Abigail," ordered Danny.

Danny was still a single man living at his workplace and his immediate family were unsure of his relationship with his extended family.

So, Danny, controversial and often despised and feared among his immediate family was doing "good deeds" for Asher, bringing him breakfast, pushing him around in the wheelchair and flattering his elderly acquaintances in the cafeteria.

In Danny's mind he was doing all these virtuous deeds for his mother, unaware his actions appeared to Abigail and Charles as though he was plotting his revenge and manipulating Asher. For the past eleven years Danny despised "the old man" and now he wanted to be a "best buddy" to the multimillionaire.

Just as he manipulated his mother with his hidden agendas and did not share the funeral arrangements with his siblings, so he would hide his scheming with Asher. Danny always came to see Asher when Charles and Abigail were not around.

Meanwhile, Charles suspected Deborah's cold shoulder toward him was because she either had negative and irrational emotions toward him or saw the dollar signs with Danny's new-found obsession with Asher.

When Charles and Abigail confronted Deborah about Danny's hidden agenda, Deborah resorted to "you have to ask

Danny about that," rather than thinking independently about the best alternative or taking a neutral position on the issues at hand.

What were the issues? The hiding of Mary's funeral arrangements, hiding Asher's trip and fall incident where Abigail was not contacted immediately, and the mysterious removal of Abigail's name form the emergency contact form. The caregiver was not contacting Abigail, as she did in the past, when she could not come to work for Asher.

In October of 2016, soon after Asher died, Charles spoke by phone to Julie, who had remained a confidante during all the previous twelve years since she introduced Mary to Asher. Charles admired Julie.

During this time, Danny was attempting to forge superficial alliances to justify his manipulation of Asher. These superficial relationships also included conversations with Asher's niece Glenda.

"Is Glenda an alcoholic?" Danny would ask Abigail in years prior, making Abigail think: *What difference does this inquiry mean to you and why are you worried about someone you hardly know?*

Also in October of 2016, Julie told Charles that Glenda spoke to Danny and that Danny stated Charles requested $100,000 to be the executor. Julie did not believe Glenda. Glenda called Charles to ask about it.

"I never, ever asked Asher for any money; not a penny!" Charles exclaimed.

Danny's claim about Charles asking for money was another lie to cover his manipulation, since Asher asked Charles to be the executor in the summer of 2015, in the kitchen. No mention of specific dollar amounts was discussed then or any other time in the future.

Charles wrote in his journal:

Last year in the month of October, of your own free will and accord, you requested me, Charles Kemp Spencer, to be the sole trustee and manager of your estate when that time comes. I was honored beyond measure of your request. The job is so important to me I am willing to perform my duties for free (no cost to your estate). Please carefully consider my request and if you are so moved by your own free will and accord, your response will be greatly appreciated.

With my best regards,
Charles Spencer

"Abigail, I have the tape recordings and the letter Asher wrote about me being the executor and power of attorney", Charles told Abigail.

Soon Charles and Abigail would put the pieces together and conclude Charles' executor job was essentially stolen by Danny aided by his attorney friend Jacky under the demise of elder abuse.

Charles exector role, derived from the serious question by Asher to the younger man, was now stolen by Danny. Not negotiated, but stolen and a moral code broken.

CHAPTER 12

THE ATTORNEYS

Charles suspected corruption by Danny due to all the time Danny was spending with Asher. But in Charles's mind, he knew his father would be disappointed if legal representation was inserted into family affairs. Donald was a kind man that settled family issues and disagreements in private with love and kindness. However, Danny was not Donald, and Charles knew family values were no more.

For the prior eleven years, Danny had despised Asher, as shown in Danny's verbal statements to Charles and Abigail. Charles and his family loved the man sincerely; in fact, they were distant from Danny due to his unpredictable comments and bitterness about the mountain property deed change. Only after Danny's mother died did Danny begin showing a regular, yet peculiar, interest in Asher's affairs.

Prior to Mary's death, Asher asked Charles to find him a local attorney, Mr. H. So, in February of 2016, four months after Mary died, Charles called the attorney representing Asher's estate. He was an older man but one thought "above reproach."

The attorney, who lived in the same retirement community as Asher, was in declining health, but was able to do the work. Charles spoke to the attorney's paralegal. The paralegal told Charles he was the executor, with power of attorney.

It was not uncommon for Asher to leave important papers on his office desk. One day, Charles had decided to snoop around Asher's desk and find his will, suspecting the will might not be the same. Asher was very private man, so asking him about his personal affairs was not something Charles would do, yet he smelled a rat and a snake.

Despite Asher's asking Charles to be the executor back in 2015, Asher failed to provide Charles a copy of the will. Charles was naturally curious. Why did Charles not ask Asher directly for a copy of the will? Was Danny nudging Asher with negative comments about Charles in attempt to get back at him?

Charles would later learn from Glenda and his aunt Joselyn that Danny was slandering Charles, so his fear of manipulation had a moral basis. Did it have a legal one?

Right there on Asher's desk, while Charles and Asher shared a glass of wine, the will had been changed without Charles's knowledge. Who was behind this action? The beneficiary cash benefit amounts were changed, and now the caregiver for Asher (Patty) was in the will. Charles took photos of the old will and the new will.

In April of 2016, Julie visited Asher. Julie, Charles, and Abigail were good friends, now having the mutual respect of Mary, Asher, and each other. They trusted each other and enjoyed each other's company.

Before Julie arrived at Asher' home, Charles, Abigail, and the 98-year-old man enjoyed some fun conversation. Then when Asher left the room, Charles noticed a manila folder which said "Will."

In the folder, Charles found yet another will and shockingly found he was no longer listed as executor. Danny was now the executor. Executors are entitled to a percentage of the estate in return for their handling of the provisions of the will. A percentage of $8 million can be quite large. In North Carolina, the maximum allowed is 5 percent, which would be $400,000.

Charles confided to Abigail and Julie about the will. Julie scolded Charles: she expected Charles to have more influence with Danny about Asher. Like Charles, Julie was unsure of Danny's motives now, due to his sudden excessive fondness for the man whom he now called "the old man."

Charles began to think he had better hire his own attorney, because Danny would be going down the path of elder manipulation and corruption.

Jacky, a 62-year-old man, was the original attorney hired by Danny to represent his mother's affairs, as written out in a simple will. Later, Danny asked Jacky to represent him as executor for Asher's estate. However, Jacky was not an estate attorney and knew very little about estate law. He is an ambulance chaser.

Do attorneys get a bad rap for poor reputation? There are good apples and bad apples, but other professions like medicine and engineering have harsh punishments for unethical practices.

Attorneys who go to extreme lengths to advertise their services directly to individuals immediately after an accident or elderly death are known as 'ambulance chasers.' These unethical professionals give a bad name to those who practice in good faith, and are a disservice to the general public because they may not realize their tactics or beliefs are really to make a quick buck.

Jacky and Danny were part of the "good old boys" network, which included men who straddled the line between good deeds and corruption in order to get paid, in cash or barter, for their services. Charles had learned while obtaining his MBA that this form of business is on shaky ground, often unethical.

Before Asher became sick, he had asked Charles to be the executor. As Asher's health declined mysteriously over several months, Danny became the executor instead – another mystery from the deep resentment Danny verbalized toward him.

The attorneys had no explanation as to why Charles's name was removed from the will. What was worse, the changes in the will were never discussed with Abigail or Charles. It became clear Danny's hidden agendas were actually corruption punishable by law.

The beneficiaries of the $9 million estate were Asher's nephews and his niece, Glenda. There were no children from Asher's marriages, so approximately 95 percent of his money and assets would go to these three.

Charles hired Keith, a long-time estate attorney, to represent him. Charles knew Danny was greedy, his "good deeds" masking selfishness and corruption.

A few years earlier, after Danny and his wife divorced, she asked Danny for one-half of the value of the home they shared. Danny would not agree to her requests. So, the ex-wife took Danny to mediation and threatened to sue him. Danny's ex-wife had to hire an attorney to resolve their asset issues, including Danny's attempt to devalue their first home.

Meanwhile, another attorney in Jacky's firm, named Jim, took over the Asher estate, or so it seemed. Charles's attorney was baffled as to why the 9-million-dollar estate and all of the paperwork were missing key issues and protocols.

In a letter to Jim, Keith outlined the issues overlooked by the Jacky and Jim firm:

Dear Jacky and Jim:

I wanted to follow up on some of the items that we discussed at your office. This obviously can get a little tricky when we have two Co-Trustees who do not get along or communicate with each other and each is separately represented.

In reviewing the Letters Testamentary, I noticed that only Danny was listed as the Trustee of the Revocable Trust, which is the beneficiary of the estate. I've spoken with the Clerk's office and they have made a notation on the estate file that Danny and Charles Spencer are the Co-Trustees of the Revocable Trust. This is necessary, as each will have to sign off on the Final Accounting when the probate estate is closed.

Up to the present time, Charles has been kept in the dark by Danny and your firm. He was not listed on the Application for Letters Testamentary as a Co-Trustee, and he believes that this was done intentionally based on suspicious practices by Danny. In an effort of good faith, I have told him that this was merely an oversight in the court paperwork that has now been rectified.

Please be aware that Charles Spencer is a "numbers guy" and takes his appointment and the fiduciary responsibility that goes with that appointment to heart. He is also aware of his potential personal liability as Trustee should there be issues with the payment of the possible estate taxes. I know that the two brothers do not get along, but because of their being Co-Trustees there must be open communication between the two of them and the three residuary trust beneficiaries.

Please let me know when the information is available to bring me up to date on the trust assets and the communication with the beneficiaries as to a good time to meet as soon as possible.

Regards,
Keith (Attorney representing Charles)

Jim's ability to carry out his duty would not hold up, as shown in the first and only attorney-client meeting. In Jim's mind and under the influence of Danny, he would manage the 9-million-dollar estate with little regard for Charles.

THE ATTORNEYS MEET

An area of conduct that is legal, yet potentially unethical, is an attorney's duty to communicate. According to the American Bar Association, a lawyer, as a member of the legal profession, is a representative of clients, an officer of the legal system, and a public citizen having special responsibility for the quality of justice.

The attorney-client privilege is a rule which prevents lawyers from testifying about, and from being forced to testify about, their clients' statements. Independent of that privilege, lawyers also owe their clients a duty of confidentiality. The duty of confidentiality prevents lawyers from informally discussing information related to their clients' cases with others. They must keep private almost all information related to representation of the client, even if that information didn't come from the client.

Keith informed Charles of the meeting they had been requesting from Jim for several weeks. Keith had discovered some serious flaws in Danny's probate filing of the will.

As previously suggested, Danny's self-image was faulty, his jealousy of Charles raging, and revenge for the mountain house deed change brewing. Thus, Danny was attempting to act like an attorney, to control everyone, but with no formal education or experience to enable him to do so.

His drinking buddy, Jacky, the first lawyer to represent Mary, had been careless in managing Asher's estate, and he left off Charles as one of co-trustees of the $9 million bank account. Charles would later learn Danny did this intentionally.

Charles began to collect information and think of legal recourses.

Soon after Charles showed up at the attorney-client meeting, Keith (representing Charles) arrived. Danny did not show up, only Jacky. Jim was waiting around in the reception area, making flattering comments about an old photo of his father and Charles's father.

The principal of the firm, Jim, attempted to appeal to Charles's emotions with the photograph of him and his father with Charles's father. Then Jim remarked about how much money was involved in the Asher estate. It became clear Jim was in the game to gain a lot of money, not for a win-win outcome.

Charles would later realize how corrupt Jacky and Jim were and the reason Danny hired a firm with either a poor reputation or an unethical firm.

Charles recalled running into Jim at the Chamber meeting back in June where he and his wife Katherine had drummed up a conversation where Jim tried to flatter Charles with his material comments about his mother Mary. Typical of a political attorney who values materialism over a family legacy.

"I really liked your mother; she was a fine lady," Jim said to Charles and Abigail while standing at the Chamber event.

At this meeting concerning Asher's estate, Charles sat on one side of the large conference room table while Jacky faced the other side. Charles put his tape recorder down on the meeting table.

"You are not going to use that, are you, Charles?" Jacky exclaimed.

Charles had learned an important lesson in note-taking in a previous job with a CEO who was forgetful. The tape recorder documented all the conversation; any future meetings had a record established without error. This legal tactic made Jacky mad and unfortunately resulted in no future-face-to-face meetings.

When a person will not meet you face-to-face to resolve an important issue, most likely he or she is hiding something.

North Carolina's wiretapping law is a "one-party consent" law. If he had not been at the meeting, Charles could not intercept or record any oral or electronic communication in the meeting. He could record this meeting since he was one of the parties and consented to it. Jacky did not consent, and it made him furious Charles would attempt to record the meeting.

When a person is defensive in negotiations or meetings, there is a good chance he or she is hiding something. Since Danny did not show up for the meeting, and there was evidence now in Charles's records that Danny manipulated Asher, by extension Jacky knew something that was likely unethical.

Jacky did not know any estate over $5.4 million was subject to the federal government tax of 40 percent. A $9 million estate would then owe $3.6 million, if the entire estate was taxed at that rate. Or, if only the portion over $5.4 million, then $0.4 \times (\$9.0 - \$5.4 \text{ million}) = \$1.44$ million. He did know that this was a big estate, and he could rake in some money just by sitting in the meeting. The "good ol' boys" were at it again.

What Danny planned was to control this money and potentially claim his mother's $2 million benefit that Asher designated for her. Because Mary died before Asher, this portability rule would not apply, and Mary's estate would get nothing.

When Asher died, Danny thought he could transfer the unused $5.4 million exclusion to Mary's estate. Keith, a longtime estate attorney set the record straight and schooled Jacky in the meeting.

"Can I use your whiteboard?" began Keith, and then he carefully and in detail wrote down the estate budget and the major tax implications. Jacky, the ambulance chaser was dumbfounded.

Jacky turned over his role to the firm's principal, Jim, who then hired an expert tax attorney.

Charles left the meeting distrusting both Jacky and Jim. Meanwhile, one of the beneficiaries was calling Charles weekly to find out when she would receive her inheritance. Months passed by. Jim would not respond formally in writing to Keith, offering instead only a casual phone call roughly monthly.

Keith sent multiple letters to Jim, getting no formal response. As Charles had learned from his business experience and academically when getting his MBA, the best way to forge solid relationships was in person. Furthermore, a service provider like an attorney owes the client a regular statement of billing hours. The billing statement of Jim's frim lacked proper organization and details.

What kind of firm does Jim manage, one that fails to disclose basic estate accounting data to Charles the co-trustee?

For Charles, attorneys were now becoming a necessary evil, playing the game of money rather than seeking the truth.

Although Keith is a "good guy," I think he is afraid to battle with Jim's firm. I *think I will fire Keith and start over. Maybe a different attorney can get Jim to be more transparent,* Charles considered.

Charles would also learn through Glenda, Asher's niece, that Danny took over Asher's affairs by cleaning out his condo in North Carolina and his home in Florida without the consent of the beneficiaries. Danny actually admitted to Glenda he should not be cleaning out the Florida high-rise condo until he officially became the executor. Another lie by Danny.

Danny made a surprise visit to Asher's Florida attorney, J.A., in another attempt to forge an alliance against Charles and Glenda. Glenda shared key information with Charles about J.A. and Danny's slanderous comments about his younger brother. Although J.A. had a good reputation in Flroida, he lacked the facts about Asher's wishes since they had not communcutaed since the executor's job was stolen by Danny. J.A. was easy prey for Danny's manipulative tactics to control the estate. "I enjoyed talking to Danny", J.A. told Glenda on the phone.

Dirty tricks in business can occur when the other side of the table does not share the agenda with whom they are negotiating. Danny and Jim were playing dirty.

Charles began to question whether law is a profession or a business. The methods used by Jim and Jacky and their client, Danny, placed professionalism and transparency, both key ethical traits of professionals on the back burner behind greed. As Jim exclaimed in the only encounter with Charles at the Chamber meeting, before he knew Charles was executor and co-trustee "I really liked your mom and there is a lot of money here." Dollar signs. Politics. Corruption.

The rules of professional conduct in law ostensibly come down on the side of law's being a profession bound by ethics, not merely a business. Charles was a professional engineer bound by a strict code of ethics. For the attorneys not to be above reproach he deemed unacceptable.

Lawyers are supposed to hold to a high standard. There must be no dishonesty; a lawyer's word has to be his bond. There can be no conflict of interest, and there can be no divided loyalties. Lawyers are fiduciaries: clients' monies held by a lawyer can't be touched. They are strictly regulated.

Were Jim, Jacky, and Danny adhering to these rules of conduct? Charles knew the answer was probably no, a disappointment for Charles, who thought his father would also be disappointed.

The original attorney, J.A., representing Asher years before Asher's marriage to Mary, was also pandered to by Danny in 2017. This attorney was to handle the sale of Asher's Florida condo, but he was careless with the paperwork, and Charles chided him by email:

> J.A. or Jim or some other attorney in the Asher Sell of Home made a trivial and unacceptable error in the settlement statement. Why can't the attorney/paralegal complete a very simple document accurately? J.A. should have known how to fill out legal documents correctly, but I think he may be a man in dotage just like Asher was. Sigh. I think I will add this doltish issue to my book I am writing, to the chapter entitled "The Attorneys."
>
> Charles

In December of 2017, Jim provided a billing statement from his firm. The first thing Charles noticed was the ledger was incomplete. Charles learned working for Lester that billing statements should have enough detail so the client knows what services were performed and how many hours were billable. But that was in the engineering profession where ethics were mandatory.

When I submit a billing statement to a client, it is itemized carefully so there is no doubt that they are paying for, thought Charles. Charles sent an email to Keith asking for permission to contact Jim directly:

Hi Keith,

I received the 12/18 accounting statement from Jim. It is not complete. By "complete" I mean that the description is not detailed, so the trustee is uninformed. For example, an 8/2/17 debit is not described. Other items missing are:

Bill paid to Funeral Home 2017 for Asher funeral—missing

Beginning balance—missing

Taxes paid not shown

Tax Attorney SB line items descriptions incomplete

Sale of Asher's property not shown

Can I respond directly to Jim? I know you are not being reimbursed for this, so I am asking to respond directly as co-trustee. Call me if you prefer.

Thanks.
Charles

Danny's attorneys, Jim and Jacky, placed a cap on how much Keith could be paid, which was likely either a controlling position by Danny or the attorney's reputation for expedient monetary gain from such a large estate. After all, Danny hired this firm because of the ease Danny would have influencing the so-called Estate attorneys.

Charles concluded Danny was a neurotic narcissist who manipulated his mother to take advantage of his father's estate after he died. And when the family farm turned into the family feud, Danny disowned his mother and spoke not to Charles. Secretly after Mary died, Danny then essentially stole the executor role of the third husband's estate from Charles using manipulation of the elderly, to gain a hefty fee the executor can get.

As the eldest son, Danny thought he deserved all of his father's assets passed down to his mother, whom he also thought he should control and win over. The problem with this thinking is it is irrational. Charles never asked his mother for part of her assets, including money or the mountain farm. The dictionary has a name for Danny's doctrine: "primogeniture."

Primogeniture is defined as the first-born male's right as the eldest son to succeed to the estate of his ancestor to the exclusion of all others. Primogeniture in ancient times was a system of inheritance in which land passed exclusively to the eldest son, partly to help keep it undivided. Until the Industrial Revolution, this system severely restricted the freedom of younger sons, who were often forced into the military or the clergy to earn a living.

Danny clearly wanted to exclude Charles from anything of monetary value in their mother's estate. On hot summer day on 2008, 7 years before the stolen executor job, Charles stopped by to see his brother hoping the older man would like a genuine chat. As typical however, Danny's terse communication and lack of empathy were evident. Charles was not fooled by Danny's words, after asking him about one of Dad's rental properties now owned by Danny. "Would you be interested in selling just one of the many properties you now own," Charles exclaimed. "Charles, you do not want those rental properties of Dad's; they are a headache," warned Danny.

If aware of it, patriarch Donald would be disappointed in Danny's behavior most of all and to a lesser extent in Deborah's and Charles's, for a variety of reasons....

CHAPTER 13

MARITAL STRIFE

In the spring of 2016, Charles launched an engineering design business in response to demands for construction firms needing building permits. Federal funding and low interest rate building loans were sparking architecture jobs, and architects needed engineers to design electrical and mechanical systems such as lighting circuits and HVAC equipment layout.

For Charles, his motivation was rooted in his entrepreneurial prowess learned from his father's repairing rental property and to a lesser extent from his experience working for a so-called "self-made" man. Actually, there is little or no evidence that successful men or women are "self-made." All the self-made men Charles knew, including CEOs, got their starts in part due to generosity or mentoring from others. Unlike brother Danny, Charles knew he would need help at some point, probably from Abigail, his faithful wife. Charles thought no one succeeds exclusively through one's own work.

Charles would apply his engineering knowledge, professional experience, and his MBA to a small business, a pure start-up with $1,000 in the bank. Charles also knew that for his business to survive, it would need a competitive advantage and effective sales and marketing. He began thinking about asking Julie to help him with ideas about the business name and marketing. Julie was the professional who introduced Mary to Asher. But Julie lived in Florida and Charles wanted to discuss his ideas with someone face to face.

To promote the business, Charles sought networking through local business groups. Charles believed face-to-face interactions would bring in more business than non-personal social media. So, the entrepreneur-engineer was thrilled to have the opportunity to tout his new business at the upcoming local commerce group's social at the local pub. Lester and Charles visited the Chamber of Commerce events.

Charles invited his wife Abigail to the Commerce Social. "Abby" was a dental hygienist who liked a "clean mouth in more ways than one." She and Charles were mostly living private lives, with little social interaction with the business community. Moreover, attending after-hours socials that included alcoholic drinks was not an activity Abigail looked forward to. She preferred sit-down dinners with family, part of the family values she had learned from her own family of seven in the 1970s and 80s. Nevertheless, she wanted to support her husband in his efforts to promote his new business.

Charles was by all accounts a decent man. He had a good reputation, as did Abigail. Both were hard-working, law-abiding, and ethical. Most people can follow common laws, but being ethical is a higher standard that raises more questions for most of the population. After all, the last twenty years has seen multiple ethical crises and deficiencies in integrity among CEOs and politicians. Bernie Madoff's Ponzi scheme resulted in billions in losses to retirees and nonprofits. The cost for citizens who were not scammed is the loss of trust created by Madoff's being able to pull off the biggest financial fraud in history right under the noses of federal regulators. Clearly, ethical leadership is lacking today.

Some would argue wrongdoing is just part of "the human condition." Charles and Abigail were taught by their parents to adhere to a moral code despite "the human condition." To use the human condition as an excuse for unethical behavior is itself inexcusable. Abigail felt this especially strongly, as she was raised in a strictly religious home.

Donald and Mary Spencer expected their children, including Charles, to abide by the moral and ethical codes; adherence to common law was not good enough. Some wonder, however: can we really teach our children to be more ethical?

Abigail had two close friends who knew Abigail as loyal, as someone who played by all the rules, including a moral code, never crossing the line.

Abby and Charles celebrated twenty-five years of marriage the previous year with only close friends and some family present. As Abigail told Charles, a marriage rededication ceremony would put her on Cloud Nine. For Abigail, the word love meant a life-long uncompromising sacrificial offering to her husband.

Charles asked Abigail to meet him at the business social after work. Abigail drove from her work by herself, meeting Charles at the pub where the social was unfolding. Several business leaders were present; finger foods and alcoholic beverages were served. Although Charles did not consider himself a drinker, he had occasionally drunk socially while traveling for a Fortune 500 firm overseas ten years prior. Abigail, on the other hand, only had a drink in private settings with her husband or with Mary or Asher.

Charles had a "pep in his step" that evening at the social event, seeking out men and women to promote his new business to. Meanwhile, Abigail was selectively speaking with a patient she saw in her dental job.

Business socials typically include a flirt, usually a man, and this evening's womanizer was Jim, an old attorney with a big ego; what he lacked in looks he made up for in charm. Abigail called for Charles to meet Jim, who reeked of vodka.

Abigail possessed the ability to detect faint smells from relatively long distances. For example, when Charles ate spicy foods for lunch, Abigail could smell his breath two feet away.

Despite Jim's efforts to entice Abigail to a drink, she adhered to her moral code, which for her included not trying to amuse men to whom a woman is not married.

"Be smart, don't start." After all, if an alcoholic did not take a first drink, they would not be an alcoholic. Similarly, if a married man does not flirt, there is a good chance he won't cheat on his wife.

Jim's wife was also present at the social, but not with Jim. Jim's drinking was nothing new; he was known around town as a controversial community activist and with unethical business practices, drinking, and flirtatious behavior that were nearly accepted by all ... until this night at the business social.

Alcohol influences your behavior in many ways. The most obvious way is that it changes your reaction to your immediate environment. Heavy drinking is dangerous, especially when you are in an unfamiliar area.

Abigail told Charles she was leaving. She was tired from work; Jim and the crowd were becoming a chore rather than enjoyment. Charles said okay and told Abigail he would be home soon.

Abigail was not Jim's only victim. Charles decided to make his rounds to see if he could market his new firm and pass out more business cards. For Charles, making personal connections had paid off in previous business ventures. On his way out the door, he ran into Jim again, who this time was flirting with Katherine.

KATHERINE

As Charles was making his way to the exit door after exchanging business cards with a few community leaders, Katherine, while talking to Jim, began smiling at Charles as though they knew each other from some previous encounter. In fact, Charles had never met Katherine before, but he did know of Jim.

Katherine and Charles exchanged looks and then started to talk. Jim retreated to a circle of women friends, only to be confronted by another man, the husband of one of the women Jim had been pouncing on during the evening's social at the bar scene. In fact, the man was more than displeased with Jim's flirtatious behavior. As Katherine engaged Charles, he saw the man pull Jim to the side. Jim and the man exchanged words. Jim is a bully which is a trait acquired from an abundant upbringing with no material need. Jim was a privileged man, never in material need and got all he wanted from his parents. Spoiled - now an alcoholic, a womanizer and a bully. But tonight Jim's big talk became small action. The woman he was flirting with had a husband who approached him "You get close to my wife again and I will beat your ass." Like a bully does, Jim was dumbfounded and left like a beat puppy dog.

Moments later, Jim's wife grabbed him and said, "Let's go, Jim!"

Katherine, an attractive, short lady in her mid-40s, asked Charles about his work and then invited him to the nearby brewery, but Charles was not a beer drinker. She also asked about the Chamber event, and he questioned her marketing prowess. Charles was attracted to Katherine's conversational skills and demeanor. As she handed him another drink of gin and tonic, his mind straddled the fence of right and wrong. But it was not alcohol that attracted Charles to her. He would later appreciate Katherine's empathy for his mother's death.

Katherine would later tell Charles she never gives out business cards, but tonight his interest made her make an exception. "Can I have your business card?", Charles asked. As the two kept eye contact, Charles noticed Katherine had a permanent freckle in her eye later learning this was likely due to some virus. In a gentle voice she explained, "I usually do not hand out business cards at social gatherings but since you asked, here is my card and my phone number is 301...". On the way home, intoxicated, he thought of her smile and attire and then called her, leaving a message. It was July of 2016.

August came, and so did multiple emails. The two exchanged information about web site design for Charles's new business. Then Katherine asked about Charles marriage, to which Charles replied, "I may be a cheater, but I will not lie to you—I am married."

Katherine responded that she was so disappointed Charles was married. Charles thought *I still need some help with my business. Who is this 45-year-old Katherine?* So, his pursuit of her continued.

Casually dressed, wearing jeans, Charles met Katherine at the sushi restaurant and brought his business papers to the restaurant, while Katherine came in a formal dress, wearing red lipstick and with a small purse. The dinner meeting turned from business discussion to an exploration of Charles's marriage.

"Are you really married, Charles?"

"Yes, I am. Remember, I told you this truth in my email. I need you to help with my business."

After sushi, Charles walked Katherine to her car, her smile suggesting she wanted more time with him; the two retreated in Charles's car for some downtown window shopping.

Charles and Katherine went to the art gallery, had another glass of wine, then Charles took her back to her car by the sushi restaurant.

"Thank you, this has been nice," said Katherine.

Charles got a letter from Katherine stating that although she really enjoyed the sushi date, she was not ready to date a married man.

"Take care," Katherine wrote, and "best of luck."

Charles replied to her in his email that he had found her antique watch in his car. After the two hugged in his car, her watch fell off and landed between the seat and the console of Charles car.

A LIE

A few days passed after the date with Katherine and Charles was still straddling the fence of good versus evil. Good was his wife and kids while evil would be to think of a single woman whom he was attracted to and emailing her.

"Dear Katherine: I really enjoyed our time. Can you help me brainstorm some marketing techniques for my new business?" Charles wrote to her. The next day after the Chamber event, Charles picked up his daughter, April at school. After sitting down in the car seat, she noticed a watch in the floorboard of Charles car. "Is this Mom's watch?", April exclaimed. Charles lied and said it was. Rather than telling the truth and avoiding future evil, Charles made a terrible decision that later would lead him down a dark path of sorrow.

Rather than mail the watch to Katherine and maintain physical separation, he texted her, saying he would drop it at her house. Katherine responded she was not at home, but he could bring it by the Wine House on Main Street...which he did.

The Wine House conversation with Katherine turned out to be another stepping stone in their attraction for each other: wine and conversation led them from the Wine House to her house. Charles dropped off the watch and Katherine was unsure of the married man but she liked his company and he house was nearby. "If you want I can stop by and see your garden", Charles asked Katherine. "Okay, but let me get ready for you - wait 15 minutes", explained Katherine. Charles had been drinking and the feeling for Katherine elevated from doing good by dropping off the watch to possibly being inside the home of an attractive single woman - not what a married man should do according to the moral code.

For the next three months Charles and Katherine would both confirm they should not be seeing each other beyond business consultations. But Charles felt something different about Katherine.

Katherine had just left a sour seven-year relationship with someone she no longer enjoyed, and the thought of getting to know a successful married man was a thrill to her, despite knowing it was not moral.

Charles's secret was his drinking and womanizing in Asia years prior, then subsequently with Katherine, until he could not keep his secret to himself. Donald had raised Charles to tell the truth, a virtue that Charles held deep inside him, but if he told Abigail the truth about Asia and Katherine, he knew she would be disappointed or worse.

CONFESSION

After Thanksgiving in 2016, Charles could hold his guilt inside of him no longer. The emotional guilt of breaking the moral code was affecting his thinking skills and, even more, he knew confession would cause a volcanic reaction with Abigail.

Later that year, a close friend asked Charles, "Don't you think by telling your wife of this affair, it was kind of selfish?"

After April left for church one Sunday evening, Charles and Abigail shared dinner. Abigail noticed Charles's eyes water, to which she responded, "What is wrong? tell me."

Charles pondered the man's statement. Then he resorted to what his father had always told him, "Tell the truth!"

Charles confessed to Abigail he first met Katherine at the Chamber event, then the next week asked her for advice on a marketing plan for his new business, then they met for sushi.

From November to March of 2017, life was hell for Abigail, Charles, and Katherine, who rode an emotional roller coaster. Charles attempted to take his life twice ... and then there was the diamond ring and a rat.

In twenty-seven years, Abigail had never taken off her diamond ring. Then it mysteriously vanished one day while she was cleaning out her car. Abigail liked a clean car, just like a clean mouth and a clean mind. Abigail had parked her new SUV in the garage. She immediately called Charles to warn him of the disappointing news. Disappointment was not what

Charles wanted to hear. Was this lost wedding ring a sign their marriage was over?

A REAL RAT

The next day, Abigail found her car seats had holes. The holes became more numerous over the next few weeks. She asked Charles about it, and he surmised that somehow a rat was entering her car. Charles placed a rat trap under the car seat. One day later, inside the car was a foul smell.

There is nothing appealing about rats. What is usually just a gross, dirty, fairly harmless species can bring death. In the 14th century, rats spread the Black Death, bubonic plague, throughout much of Europe and parts of Asia.

Although the rat trapped in Abigail's car was not even close to becoming a pandemic, it seemed strange and symbolic of something, or someone, bringing a distasteful presence in her marriage.

A METAPHORICAL RAT

Abigail felt Charles was being a rat during this time of the affair—his mind sometimes with Katherine and sometimes with his wife, dual allegiances.

Charles was secretive, detached, and betraying Abigail.

Rats are scary, and Charles was frightening Abigail. But rats are survivors, able to withstand harsh environments. The rats flourished in Abigail's garage and in her SUV, while Charles was learning to survive on his own. Down deep inside of him, and in her soul, she could not accept that their marriage was over.

Katherine was the only woman Charles had ever met with whom he would break his moral code. Women and men who abide by a moral code do not engage in a relationship, beyond friendship, with someone of the opposite sex. Furthermore, moral men don't have "friends with benefits." Charles felt himself to be in a deep hole, needing help. Katherine was sympathetic toward Charles. He soaked up her tender words, but she was the last person he needed to restore his marriage. The one person he did need, Abigail, now could not help him.

CHAPTER 14

THE PSYCHOLOGIST

At the suggestion of Charles's best friend, Bobby, Charles sought the advice of an eminent psychologist about the crisis and the brewing emotional turmoil. The crisis had left Abigail wounded deeply and Charles confused, although confusion was not his only emotional pain.

Charles and Abigail visited Dr. M., the psychologist, on November 30, 2016. Arriving at Dr. M.'s office, they noted his impressive license to practice hung next to his office in the foyer. Over the intercom played romantic and soft jazz music with a dose of the DJ Delilah.

The sounds were not even close to creating any hint of solitude. Abigail's heart was now on life support; Charles's behavior was frantic with implicit pleas for help, yet he was still emotionally attached to Katherine.

Charles and Abigail were unsure what to expect from Dr. M. He had a grand reputation. His clients were said to include CEOs and governmental leaders.

"Abigail, Charles, come on in. First, I must ask you to be totally honest in order for me to help you," said Dr. M.

Dr. M's demeanor reminded Charles of one of his college professors, and his listening skills seemed similar to those of his father, a man of few words but an excellent listener—just what Charles had needed growing up.

Dr. M, a tall, dark-haired man, appeared to be in his early sixties. Charles came to learn he served in the Vietnam War as a clinical psychology intern to the severely wounded after they were relocated to Hawaii.

Abigail cried during the one-hour counseling session. Dr, M. announced some disappointing news that made Abigail cry even more, "The only way this marriage will survive is if you both put energy into the relationship. A marriage does not thrive by turning on the autopilot."

Abigail did not want to hear this, since she had worked hard to honor Charles for twenty-seven years. The couple left with Abigail unsatisfied. Charles, on the other hand, would grow to like the psychologist.

During the following year, in one of the dozen sessions in which Charles participated, Dr. M. told Charles about a Vietnam vet who lost his legs, penis, and testicles in the Vietnam War but managed to fall in love with a woman who remained devoted to this disabled man. This story would make an impact on Charles's thinking about marriage, commitment and "truth in love."

Charles thought, Abigail has stayed by my side for nearly twenty-seven years. Why can I not cut off this demon?

Charles gained a greater appreciation of how the brain works from interacting with Dr. M., not from a neurological biology standpoint, but from the basic functions of thoughts, emotions, and behavior. By this time, Charles's behavior toward Abigail and his family had become unstable, erratic, overly emotional.

Thoughts, emotions, behavior—these are the mind's cognitive process elements.

Thoughts—*I care for my family, but I enjoy the conversations with Katherine.*

Thoughts—*I am really in a deep hole now, having broken the moral code, having told Abigail the truth and yet lying to my best friend, Bobby, in the process.*

Thoughts—*Do Katherine and I have a future? The statistics say no. I don't have to sleep with Katherine. The conversations at her dinner table alone are so therapeutic.*

Thoughts—*Is this whole crisis a bad dream. Dreams? Shattered dreams?*

Thoughts—*What would Mary think? Oh, how Donald would be so disappointed in me!*

Dr. M. inquired of Charles, "Why did you break your moral code? What were you thinking? Tell me what series of events led up to this."

Charles learned from his long-time faithful friend, Bobby, that the psychologist had lost his only son to a tragic tree accident. Charles concluded that Dr. M., a Vietnam veteran, highly intelligent, was a man who could relate to his crisis.

Unlike some psychologists who prescribe theoretical remedies, Dr. M. was wise in his practical remedies for Charles. In one session, Dr. M., with a straight face and a direct tone, asked Charles why he liked to look at "morsels outside his home," when in fact "all the sweet goodness was right there in front of you."

Dr. M. focused on an answer to his first question, which was that there was some void in Charles's life, and it was the reason he broke his own moral code. The moral code to Charles was a tenet passed down to him from Donald, which included the law of honesty, the law of work ("if you don't work, you don't eat"), and the law of respect (respect those around you, especially your elders and family members).

"How about discipline?" asked Charles.

"Discipline is important, Charles, to keep you from looking for morsels outside your own home," exclaimed Dr. M.

Charles thought to himself, *but discipline is something I have been doing most of my life. I run 25 miles a week, rise at 6 a.m., work hard, advance my education, invest for profits in my savings account, help others. What more do I need to be disciplined about?*

Charles acknowledged to Dr. M. that there were multiple unresolved issues bothering him, including the mountain house deed, the lack of cooperation with Danny, superficial talk with his siblings, and to a lesser extent the issues surrounding Asher and Mary's estate.

Charles told Dr. M. that he sent a personal letter to both of his siblings in an attempt to understand their hidden agendas, such as hiding some information about Mary's funeral and, to a lesser extent, hiding her assets and estate matters. Charles told Dr. M. his only complaint about his mother's executor was that Danny had not been transparent in explaining the estate and will process.

Dr. M. said the letter represented a formal communication to meet and discuss the issues, and if Charles had been genuine in the correspondence, nothing more can be done.

Deborah's husband sent an email in October of 2016 to arrange a meeting with Mary's children; however, Charles replied he would attend the meeting with his attorney present, a response that offended Deborah.

Charles told Dr. M. he hired an attorney because Danny could not be trusted, having exhibited a lack of communication and transparency. Charles was convinced that prudence dictated he use an attorney in legally complicated family affairs.

Charles thought, *I don't hate my siblings, but their behavior demands I protect myself legally. After all, families are worse than friends when it comes to money.*

Dr. M. and Charles agreed there was a "void" in his life: a lack of family unity and the loss of the dream Mary experienced with her first two husbands. Charles told Dr. M. he felt the family disunity and the unethical behavior of Danny toward Asher, as well as Mary's declining health, caused some emotional pain.

But the reason Charles went out of his home to find "another sweet morsel" when a healthy meal was before him was still a mystery...or was it?

Dr. M. exclaimed many times, "How important is this marriage to you? The answer dictates how much work has to be done."

Charles was intent on taking notes, while Dr. M stared directly at his client/subject. "You cannot have 'dual allegiances,' to Katherine and your family. You are about to lose both if you do not make a decision and make it swiftly."

The hardest question the psychologist posed to Charles was not "Do you love Abigail?" but "Why do you want to be married to Abigail?"

Charles was dumbfounded. He had not considered this question since their engagement in 1988.

Christmas would be coming soon, and Charles knew his family time would be strained. Dr. M. suggested he write a speech and give it to his family.

Charles and Abigail agreed they each would write their own speech and give it to the children on Christmas Day 2016.

Dr. M. had little empathy for Charles. He knew Charles was not diagnosed with any clinical psychological problems, only high anxiety, and was prescribed the common drug, Buspirone.

Charles had thought, *I really need some man like Dr. M. to set me straight. What man can do it?*

Buspirone is an anti-anxiety medicine that affects chemicals in the brain that cause anxiety. Buspirone is used to treat symptoms of anxiety, such as fear, tension, irritability, dizziness, pounding heartbeat, and other physical symptoms.

Charles concluded, after four weeks of Buspirone, that there was no measurable effect on his behavior. "I really don't need this medicine. I prefer natural remedies."

Would Charles's behavior improve by using some other remedy? Charles's remedy would be an addiction to the soft-spoken words of Katherine, the never-married woman who liked poetry, art museums, and cuddling.

Charles believed that if his father were around, he would take Charles out back behind the shed and beat his backside, giving him what is known as a "whooping."

For Charles, none of the men he had encountered in the previous 20 years appeared to be the kind of role model he needed to hold him accountable and challenge him to be a strong moral man.

Dr. M. reminded him, "to have a friend, you must be one."

Meanwhile, Dr. M. helped Charles outline the Christmas speech, which read something like the following:

December 25, 2016

Dear Family,

For the past few months, I have allowed selfish, immoral behavior to come into my life unchecked. I distanced my thoughts away from your mother. I deeply regret this now. I had an affair with another woman. I caused great pain to her and you. I broke our wedding vows and want to apologize to you. Mom and I are talking and deciding the best course of action.

We each love you,
Dad

Charles thought, *the void can only be filled after deep introspection about "who you are and whose you are."*

"Going deep" was mandatory for a marriage to thrive, according to Dr. M., and he explained to Abigail and Charles that in order for an apple not to rot, you must take care of it, "If you place an apple in the refrigerator, it can survive for a long time. Your marriage is like an apple. If you do not nurture it, the apple will die."

As Dr. M. sat in his chair, his body erect, hands coming together much like a child praying, his eyes intent and focused toward Charles, he inquired, "Why did you try to kill yourself, Charles?"

Charles looked at Dr. M. and said rather casually: "It was two-fold; I was desperate for relief, and I wanted to get to Abigail somehow ... which was manipulation".

Charles explained a series of events that had occurred over the course of three days that wounded Abigail deeply.

During December, Katherine left a present for Charles at his office downtown, on the steps outside. Katherine sent text messages Charles frequently, and Charles enjoyed the flattery, or so he thought. But over the holidays, Katherine and Charles agreed to not contact each other.

"Give yourself some time—you really need to think though all of this," Katherine explained to Charles. "I feel for you, but you lied to me that there was little hope for your marriage."

In fact, at that point, Charles did hold little hope for the marriage.

Charles was bothered by Abigail's unwillingness to talk and try to fix the crisis. Charles was an engineer, and like an engineer, he wanted to redesign and fix the marriage. Charles would later learn a hard lesson that he alone would never be able to "fix" a broken heart.

Katherine and Charles, despite agreeing to stop all communication, managed to rekindle their intense passionate written words repeatedly for several months. They seemed unable to keep from doing this. Katherine fueled the flames of passion with consistent empathy for Charles's void.

Charles wrote in his journal:

I still have limerence[1] for Katherine since she remains in my thoughts. She is in my thoughts because I shared a large amount of information about me and my family, especially

---

1   Limerence is the state of being infatuated or obsessed with another person, typically experienced involuntarily and characterized by a strong desire for reciprocation of one's feelings but not primarily for a sexual relationship.[1]

the deaths of Mary and Asher, and she confided in me. Like my mother, she had cancer and I enjoy her conversation topics and the hugs. In front of my wife, she told me she loved me on Valentine's Day, and I believed her. She likes to go to art museums and take nature walks. She likes to read poetry and she speaks softly and is cute. She has never raised her voice at me. Stupid me, this is all fantasy, but she enables my thoughts to believe something real and new and exciting could happen. But why am I not satisfied with Abigail?

There is no scientific or moral basis for maintaining limerence for Katherine. It is a waste of time since the outcome is proven almost fruitless. Limerence is a cycle of confusion for me.

Damn, I am so confused.

The weekend of December 3rd Charles took Katherine to see Rainbow's End and Katherine was in awe of the place. Then the following Monday, Charles and Katherine met over dinner at a Indian Restaurant. The two had grown to like exotic foods and talk about 80s music and art. But the underlying issue was where was this relationship heading after five months as an immoral affair. Katherine thought to herself "He really does care for me, but will it last?" The two hugged over dinner and talked about their relationship, specifically where it was heading. "That is Venus", Charles said as he pointed in the sky as the two walked back to their cars.

Charles always met Katherine out of town, so no friends would see him breaking the moral code or suspect an affair. Unfortunately, Charles's emotion of shame was weaker than his limerence for her.

On this night, Charles finished the meal with Katherine and headed home, leading Katherine until she would take a two-mile detour before he exited down his main road; all was well, so he thought.

As Katherine took a turn to her house, Charles turned down his main road, only to see Abigail parked on a side street.

Charles pulled onto his home's driveway. Surprisingly, Abigail pulled in behind him. Then Abigail rolled her window down and at the same time, drove into the garage, saying, "You have made your decision. You are not welcome here."

LOCKED OUT

One negative genetic trait Charles had in common with his birth family was stubbornness and emotional reactions rather than rational thinking. As Charles attempted to enter his home, Abigail locked the door and kept the key.

Charles was devastated.

To Abigail's claim that Charles had made the decision to stay with Katherine, he exclaimed, "I have not made my decision!"

Charles was distressed once again with conflicting emotions. This time, he knew Abigail was serious. She wouldn't talk. She had given him a chance to change, and he did not.

A few months later, Charles learned that Abigail had walked into the house, turned off all the lights, and fell on the basement couch, crying in pain, the kind of pain that causes nausea, not due to the stomach disorder but to a broken heart.

Their fifteen-year-old daughter, April, asked, "Mom, what is wrong? Are you pregnant? Why are you crying?"

Charles could not gain entry to his home. He knew he had every right to be in his home, legally, but not the way their marriage was, and he wanted to talk to Abigail. He had not learned that sometimes it is best to not speak, better to leave the wounded alone. Abigail wanted no part of the man she knew was still questioning who he was.

With nowhere to go, ashamed, confused, chilled by the cold wintry air, Charles walked a few miles. Walking the empty streets was something Charles did hoping something, or someone, would inspire him and change his thinking and behavior.

"Fight or flight" kicked in.

Charles fled to the one who had been so understanding and patient with him during the crisis he created—Katherine. He called her. She asked what was wrong, to which he replied, "I cannot get into my house—she threw me out."

"You can come over to my place—I have logs on the fire and wine," said Katherine.

Charles arrived at Katherine's home, a cozy two-bedroom villa about ten minutes away. Charles explained what happened. Katherine convinced him he needed a good night's sleep.

After drinking a few glasses of Merlot and listening to some jazz, Charles stayed at Katherine's house that night. Katherine would once again take the rollercoaster ride of emotions for Charles.

Charles's sleep was disrupted by confusion on December 7, Pearl Harbor Day, at 4 a.m. Katherine comforted him with a hug. Often, sleep would not come during this crisis; besides, Charles did not sleep well away from home.

Charles awakened Katherine again at 7:30 a.m. "What's wrong - are you okay?" Katherine said. Charles responded quietly holding back tears, "I have no idea what this day holds for me. I'm locked out of my house and the life I knew may be over."

Abigail forbade Charles' presence at his home. Katherine was empathetic and hopeful their six-month romantic relationship would take on a new meaning now with Charles no longer wanted by Abigail.

At Rainbow's End, with the enchanted forest surrounding her, Katherine's heart had fallen for Charles, despite her continual concern of not breaking the moral code with a married man.

Charles decided to visit his home at 9 a.m. to get some clothes to prepare for sleeping in a hotel. He got there, and the main door was double-locked, keeping him stranded outside. Abigail instructed April and Ashland to make sure the house was double-locked.

Infuriated, Charles broke the glass at the back door. Donald had taught Charles how to repair glass and doors. His emotions overcame him once inside the house.

At home, all alone, with family photos abounding, something, some emotion, something divine entered Charles's heart and soul. Then he discovered on her nightstand what Abigail had written only a few days prior:

Dear Charles,

I have always loved you and I always will. But I cannot keep living like this. When you were with the other woman, I was not cursing you or plotting my revenge. I was on my knees praying to God and He comforted me. He alone gave me peace. So, I do not need you now, for God is my refuge. He is my fortress and my comforter.

Abigail

Charles thought to himself: "Do I want to risk it all for Katherine?" What Charles did not understand was that two human beings who are 'in love' can not really know each other in 3 months or even 6 months even when they have thought about having a future long term relationship. Then he thought of Donald and Mary who believed Abigail was an angel. Divine intervention would later convince Charles.

Charles thought, *you cannot do this to yourself and your family. You are destroying yourself and the life you once knew.*

Desperate, Charles cried and called Ashland, who was not only the preacher's wife, Abigail's friend, but more importantly the "second mom" of Charles's youngest daughter, April. "Second mom" was the half-joking, half-serious slang term given to Ashland for her dedication in carpools and school functions that often aided Abigail.

"You need some help, Charles. I will call Eddie to come

over and see you."

Eddie, Ashland's husband, served as the preacher where April attended church regularly. April had become a close friend to Eddie's family.

Eddie arrived and confronted Charles, "Have you been drinking alcohol?"

Charles responded, "This is not a drinking problem. There is another woman in my life. I need to fix this now or die."

Eddie asked Charles for his *Bible*. Charles fumbled, only to find *The Bible Handbook*. *The Bible Handbook* contained a moral code, but Eddie preferred the King James Version of the *Holy Bible*.

Eddie found a *Bible* and quoted some scripture, dealing with "the woman at the well" (*John 4:* 4–26). Jesus upbraided the woman for having had five husbands and living with a man who was not her husband. Eddie also quoted Jesus's words from the story of a woman who was about to be stoned for the sin of adultery, "Let he without sin cast the first stone" (*John 8:* 1-11), and said how none of her accusers met that rigorous requirement.

Then, Jesus told the adulterous woman, "Neither do I condemn you; go, and from now on, sin no more" (*John 8:* 10-11).

Eddie told Charles to break off all communication with Katherine. "You may be saved, but you are practicing sin. We all are sinful, but practicing sin will separate you from God."

Charles texted Bobby to come to his home. After an hour, Eddie and Charles talked. Bobby was on his way there. Bobby arrived, and the three men prayed to God to purge Charles of his sinful behavior. Bobby challenged Charles to call Katherine immediately and tell her it was over.

"Charles, you have limerence for Katherine. The sex may be great, but it is just sex. You are going to be sorry one day, and your life will be miserable alone," Bobby advised.

In tears, Charles called Katherine, saying, "I am sorry, but it is over."

Katherine replied, "Charles, Charles, what do you mean?"
There was silence. Charles hung up the phone.

Charles repaired the broken glass door just as Donald had taught him. Shattered glass symbolized shattered dreams.

FINISHED?

On Pearl Harbor Day, at the end of his rope, Charles was contrite and sorrowful. He had no clue on this day divine inspiration would not nullify the relationship with Katherine. Charles did not foresee that this relationship would last yet another three months.

Over the next month, Charles explained to his children why their mother was in despair. On Christmas Eve, the children learned of the affair. Charles gave the speech to the children and everyone cried. The once pure bond and sacred vow had become a dirty rope dangling in the wind.

Charles slept downstairs on the couch.

He told his best friend Bobby he had no contact with Katherine, having written her a letter of rejection. In fact, Charles had lied to Bobby, since he secretly wrote another letter to Katherine, pleading to remain friends. Katherine had been distraught until she received the second letter.

Confusion had confounded Charles throughout the month of December.

RAGE, DEMONIC RAGE?

To make matters worse, Abigail's broken heart would be defended by her anger and rage. On a cold wintry night, Abigail threatened Charles to the point of assault. Charles believed that either Abigail was a different person now or there was some demonic spirit in his office while his wife was present.

Demons were an idea Charles dismissed until that cold night. He never saw a demon, only read about them in the *Bible*. Plus, the *Bible* says that Satan can oppress, tempt, slander, and accuse a person. But a Christian who is indwelled by the Holy Spirit cannot be possessed by a demon. "Where the Spirit of the Lord is, there is liberty" (*2 Cor. 3*:17).

Abigail showed up at Charles' office. He had been living on pins and needles between Abigail's spontaneous threats to Katherine's text messages.

So on a cold wintry night with snow falling, Abigail knocked on Charles's office door. "Where is she!" Abigail yelled. Charles had learned you don't fight with an angry woman especially your wife. "Abigail please, I am trying to get some work done", he pleaded.

The work Charles was doing was thinking: "How can I fix this enormous problem?"

Charles was already anxious that day, fearful of what Abigail might find in his office. The birthday presents Katherine had left for him, Abigail and Charles had agreed to destroy. But Charles kept a few of Katherine's mementos in his office. He was still hanging on to Katherine.

Abigail started walking around the office, snooping through the closet and found a present. She confronted Charles, "Are there any other presents of hers in your office?"

Charles tried to avoid this confrontation, saying, "there are no more presents from her," continuing his work on the computer. Charles knew full well Katherine had also left him a book and some cookies which were secretly tucked away inside his desk, not in the closet where Abigail exclaimed: "I'm going to go to her house and find out if she loves you!"

Charles pleaded with Abigail, fumbling with his phone texting to warn his lover Katherine and yelling "No don't go see her, we can work this out Abigail!"

Abigail did not stop in the closet looking for evidence of the love affair, then there was Charle's torn up love letter to

Katherine in his trash can.

Abigail was smart. She saw the trash can was full of papers all torn up. She turned the trash can over in the neat office and started going through the papers. Charles knew he was caught, thinking, *when am I going to stop lying? White lies or black lies, they need to stop. Either she will kill me, or I am going to ruin my life!*

In a fit of rage, Abigail saw the name "Katherine" on a small piece of paper, then the birthday card. Finally, she pieced together a love letter.

"Is this it, or is there more of her?" demanded Abigail. "I found it. You are a liar. I am going to call Bobby and tell him you are lying. You still love her!" Abigail rebuked Charles.

Charles left his *Bible* on the office side table. By now, this holy book was only an empty symbol to Abigail, not anything close to representing Godliness on the part of Charles. *Who is this man who use to pray with me and love me and has now become an unstable cheater?* she thought.

Abigail was furious while pacing the room like a lion looking to devour anything that got in her way. The once kind and gentle lady was obviuos to Charles a different person and he now feared her.

"Turn around! Look at me! You are not the Godly man you think you are. Satan has infested you and I am going to stop you and her!" shouted Abigail.

By now Abigail's voice was not the soft gentle tone Charles new for the past 25 years, but a deep and strong angry voice.

The broomstick that was in the closet was now in Abigail's hand. "Now take this"! Abigail yelled as she pushed the stick across his neck making Charles fall to the floor.

Charles now feared for his physical safety.

Abigail exclaimed, "You see that Bible over there? Have you read it? Recite to me the Psalms where David committed adultery with Bathsheba". "Now! Recite it now or die!" exclaimed Abigail to Charles with the broomstick pressing on his neck lying on his back.

Charles would later believe and assert that Abigail, the meek and mild, kind woman who knew no hatred, unleashed a fit of rage that changed her voice and led her to violence, perhaps due to a demonic spirit that enabled her to grab a broom stick and attack Charles.

Was Abigail really invaded by the Devil that night when assaulting Charles?

Charles assertion is counter to the *Bible*'s teaching. There is no clear example in the *Bible* where a demon ever inhabited or invaded a true believer. Abigail was a born-again Christian, and her life had always shown it. Never in the New Testament epistles are believers warned about the possibility of being inhabited by demons.

That cold night in his office, he took a beating.

He later told Bobby, "Donald taught me by his example toward Mary, to never, ever hit a woman, and I did not. I took my beating."

The beating did not change Charles.

Christmas would come soon. Instead of the hope of Jesus in Charles's mind and heart, as in previous Christmases, his soul was dirty, his mind tormented.

Christmas lights and ornaments did not get hung. On December 17, at 3:40 p.m., Charles received a text message from Katherine: she wanted to break it off. Prior to getting this message from Katherine, Charles received a text message from Abigail that she needed more time to think about things.

In a state of despair, Charles frantically left his office, headed for the railroad station three blocks away. For Charles, most of his emotions were despair and manipulation. *How can I get Abigail's attention that I am desperate for an answer?*

Abigail had told Charles, "I cannot help you."

ENDING IT

"I cannot help you" to Charles meant Abigail was quitting. Quitting was no longer acceptable to Charles, who had struggled with quitting important activities in his youth. Charles would surmise that "quitting life" may be less painful than a divorce or losing both Abigail and Katherine.

So, Charles sent a text message to Abigail while walking to the railroad tracks: "I am going to end all of this nonsense. I am going to the railroad tracks downtown."

Over the next ten minutes, Charles walked up and down the tracks. He recalled what a work colleague railroad engineer told him in Los Angeles about suicide. The engineer said that the suicides he witnessed occurred on "tracks of tears," as homeless folk would fall near the tracks and be mangled or killed. "The victims just lay down and died right in front of my eyes."

But Charles could only think about the mess he was in and why Abigail would not talk to him. He also thought, *is this Katherine all worth this pain? Who was she really? Life cannot go on with this crisis.*

On his cell phone, the police called him. Abigail called him. Charles sent the calls to voice mail.

His response mixed desperation and manipulation, at the expense of family and friends.

Then, he heard Abigail calling from afar, from atop the hill overlooking the tracks hidden by the station platform. "I never said it was over; I love you! I do!"

The words were all Charles needed to hear. Why had he not realized Abigail had a deep, abiding love for him? He made a path to the right-of-way, up the hill to the outstretched arms of Abigail.

WHY SUICIDAL?

We return to Dr. M.'s question of why Charles wanted to commit suicide.

Charles responded: "I would be lying if I said it was free of some manipulation, but it was also desperation. My emotional state was driving my decisions rather than thinking about good things that would drive acceptable behavior. I am desperate to fix this crisis. I am an engineer—I like to fix things."

Manipulation was a behavior Abigail knew full well, even before the episode with Charles. Abigail was one of the few family members who knew Danny was a manipulator, especially with his mother.

Unlike his father, Danny liked to bargain with people in the fashion of, "I'll scratch your back, if you will scratch mine."

Danny would pretend to be nearly desperate for money, telling his mother he was broke or complaining about family monetary needs.

Dr. M. told Charles that there was no quick fix to this crisis. "You have wounded your wife deeply, and the best thing you can do is give her space. If she is willing to forgive you and put some energy back into the marriage, it can survive."

Charles slept in the home's basement during this time. Often, he would be awakened by Abigail who was angry. One early morning at 3 a.m. Abigail woke Charles to confront him about Katherine. She demanded answers and ridiculed Charles for breaking the vow.

Then two days later, Abigail came to see Charles in the middle of the night seeking solace and affection, the two holding each other for hours. The next morning Charles found this note on his bedside table:

1-6-17

Charles,

My love for you has not changed. At this moment as I write I am hurting and I am seeking God's wisdom and guidance. I kindly ask you not to pressure me or force me to do something I am not willing to do or say. I am willing to allow you to stay in this house, but boundaries have to be in place. I am aware of the promises you made to me, but there has to be no contact with Katherine or any other woman. Contact includes email, phone, letters, and personal meetings. If this happens we will separate, and I will ask you to leave. I am willing to pray for and with you.

The next few weeks, months and years will be challenging, but we need patience as we allow God to have His way in our lives.

Much love,
Abigail

Charles then wrote letters, including this one for his wife Abigail, in which he included a poem he wrote:

Life can hurt.
It just hurts.
What was once a crystal mass
Pouring love and life
Has been knocked and broken and
Is now just a dangerous piece of broken glass.

But glass can flow and bend.
It shall return after a mend.
I guess it's true:
Hurt people, hurt people too."

BACKSLIDING

Instead of a resolution of the crisis, Valentine's Day came, and so did a date with Katherine. When Charles came home that night, he resorted to the basement couch, still confused, desperate for answers and lacking a deep conviction to change. The flattery, physical comfort, and text messages from Katherine were meeting a deep emotional desire.

Charles feared to be in his home now. He could hardly hide

there. Abigail would dictate any activity around the house, including asking probing questions and making threats.

Abigail came down from her upstairs bedroom and asked, "Did you have any contact with her?"

Charles responded that he had, which incensed Abigail, who issued verbal threats that escalated to a physical altercation.

Charles would never assault Abigail because of Donald's loving example for his wife. Men tend to care for their wives according to the degree of the positive role models of their parents, which both Charles and Abigail were fortunate to experience in their youth.

Rather than being quiet and sleeping on the disagreement, Charles left the house and stayed at his office for the night. The next day he visited psychologist Dr. M.

Dr. M. explained to Charles he was in a "fight or flight" mode of thinking. Our brain's autopilot system responds to our emotions and intuitions. Its cognitive processes take place in the part of the brain that developed early in childhood. This system guides our daily habits, helps us make snap decisions, and reacts instantly to dangerous life-and-death situations (such as saber-toothed tigers) through the freeze, fight, or flight stress response.

While it helped Charles survive in the past, the fight-or-flight response was not the best response to help resolve the moral crisis Charles had caused. Abigail was "done with Charles," at least these were her words. But was she really the kind of woman who would separate and seek to divorce Charles for his behavior?

Meanwhile, Charles attempted to perform as a teacher at work, while still in some contact with Katherine. Once-hourly texts sent from Katherine were now sent daily. Then he received a text from his oldest daughter, Savannah.

Dad,

Until you get yourself straightened out, there is no reason to keep sending text messages requesting a dinner date. Stop the bullshit. If you want the other woman, then leave Mom alone and go to the other person. Mom is awesome! She is kind, a special lady and awesome. Please make up your mind.

Savannah

THE PSYCH WARD

In March 2017, Charles spent an hour with Dr. M. During the session, Charles knew his doctor completely understood the crisis. Charles also thought to himself, *Dr. M. has provided a deep nugget of information I can use to get rid of Katherine.*

The "nugget," as Charles understood it, was a word he borrowed from his research advisor Dr. Y., who told Charles to find something new and deep in his study of optical pulses, something which would require some digging, a nugget. On this evening, another doctor, Dr. M., provided a nugget to help Charles to get rid of Katherine.

Was it "backbone" or courage that Charles needed to rid himself of this distracting woman? This woman he met at the Chamber meeting had managed to steal part of his heart and confuse him for several months.

Dr. M. would ask the same deep question over and over again: "Why do you want to be married to Abigail?"

Charles was confused. He knew it. He decided to write down all his thoughts in a journal. He kept the journal on his computer because he did not want anyone to find his letters. He feared it might be found by Abigail, who had already found one love letter to Katherine, a letter which incited an intense altercation in December of 2016.

Nevertheless, Charles thought to himself: *why did I get myself into this mess and what would Donald think? Can I still keep his dream alive? Have I screwed up so badly I am just another statistic in the world of broken families?*

Charles penned his answer to the deep question about marriage in his journal:

Why do I want to be married to Abigail? There are many personality traits and character qualities that Abigail possesses that make her an excellent wife and mother. I admire her work ethic. I recently have admired again her physical attributes and her newly-found goal of running a marathon. She is devoted to her family. She told me her legacy was our children. Yet Danny did not accept the real legacy of Donald's dream.

Despite my terrible behavior, Abigail told me she still loves me, and I believe her. She is truly committed to the marriage. But over the last years, the marriage did not add to my self-worth, although there were moments of enjoyment. She was not "making me happy"—happiness is a choice, but your partner can influence it by what is said. (Do others make one happy? I thought I was in control of my own happiness.) I started to compare the marriage against a morsel of affection and tenderness from someone else. But these traits of Abigail are not the reasons I want to be married to her. There is no other woman that will meet my needs like Abigail since she knows my being better than anyone else. (She has lived with me for twenty-eight years.) She will be there for me when I am old. We can have a decent retirement together. She can help me with my business. Will my children be better off if I remain married to Abigail?

Dr. M. went on to say, "There are zero guarantees for this marriage and Abigail's response to you."

The psychologist chided Charles, "The relationship with Katherine is built on a lie, the lie that she and you believe about marriage. You lied to Katherine and Abigail. Focus on today, not yesterday nor tomorrow. You do not know if tomorrow will come. Marriage was meant for two people, not three. Statistically speaking, Charles, if you continue on with this relationship with Katherine, you have at best a ten percent chance of courtship and even less at a happy marriage.

"Your homework for the next week is 1) be kind to your family, especially Abigail; 2) decide how important this marriage is to you; and 3) go to the basement."

"Going to the basement" was the term Dr. M. gave to the mental exercise of thinking hard and deep about questions such as, "Who am I?" and "What is the void you felt when you strayed?" as well as "What is really important to me?"

However, this homework would not be turned in ... because of another crisis.

SUICIDE ATTEMPT NO. 2

As Charles sat in his car on a cold Tuesday night, he called Katherine to ask her to never contact him again. "Married men do not do this with single women. And single women do not hang out with married men," Charles explained.

Katherine agreed, but she wanted to meet Charles in person to say goodbye. In the interim, Charles told Abigail he was with Dr. M. and would be home around 7:30 that night, after spending an hour at his office.

Charles and Katherine met for Indian food a few miles from her home.... Driving in separate cars, Charles then headed for his office.

Charles stopped by his office after the dinner date with Katherine. Katherine invited Charles over for cocktails. Charles knew he had to prove his trust again and needed to tell Abigail where he was and what he was doing. Unfortunately, a split-second decision Charles made, not telling the truth, would create chaos this night.

Charles's behavior was so out of the ordinary. He would walk to Katherine's house from his office rather than taking his car. The night was cold, and he was looking forward to the warm fire and a glass of wine.

Arriving at Katherine's home, Charles turned his phone off, only to find, 30 minutes later, Abigail had been calling and texting him multiple times.

Abigail's last text message read: "There has been some indiscretion tonight. Do not come home ever again."

Fight-or-flight kicked into Charles brain.

These were words Charles heard once before, when he found Abigail running at the track one night. Charles had told her he was proud of her running, to which she replied, "I'm done; do not come home."

"Bye, Katherine." Charles grabbed his belongings and ran back to his office.

These were the last words from Charles that Katherine would ever hear.

Arriving at home intoxicated, Charles attempted to pick Abigail up and take her with him. Abigail's youngest daughter, April, was distraught. Abigail had been talking to Bobby on the phone.

"Give me the phone," said Charles.

Charles and his buddy Bobby exchanged some inflammatory words.

The next day, suicide attempt two occurred. Abigail was feeling manipulated by Charles's intensity to gain information about her. The "fight" element was just as strong as "flight" for Charles. However, Abigail felt threatened by his suicide threats.

Mental illnesses often come with the risk of suicide. But Charles's diagnoses by the psychologist and the psychiatrist at the hospital had revealed anxiety and emotional confusion, not clinical depression or illness.

Some diagnoses, such as borderline personality disorder, come with a ten percent suicide completion rate, although there are often many attempts that are unsuccessful or are simply exaggerated cries for help. Other disorders, including depression, eating disorders, and substance abuse, carry suicide risks as well.

Abigail was deeply concerned, but she was also tired of all the chaos. She had never encountered suicide, but she knew to take threats seriously and to follow through with calling for help.

Unfortunately, she was now on the receiving end of constant manipulation and threats, and her desire to help Charles turned to anger and resentment. Being constantly bombarded by comments from Charles about threatening to kill himself was emotional blackmail. Abigail did not know what would come next, and as a result, feelings of anger, resentment, and fear were building up.

What will he do next? Will he leave me? Abigail thought. Would he leave twenty-eight years of marriage for someone he knew for six months?

So, after a three-mile run, Abigail asked Charles not to come home. Instead of doing as she'd asked, Charles parked his car a few blocks away and walked home, then lay down on the living room floor, his mind and body exhausted from all the commotion.

Charles wanted information about Abigail: *What is she thinking?*

Abigail phoned Charles. He had his phone next to him, as he lay in the darkened living room under a couch. "Charles, what are you doing? I asked you to leave."

Abigail called Ashland for help, not sure if Charles would be angry again.

Rather than hiding, fearing rejection, Charles marched up to Abigail, who was waiting for Ashland in the driveway.

"What is wrong with you? Why do you want to talk to me?" shouted Charles.

"I want you out of my life!" exclaimed Abigail.

At that moment Charles heart dropped.

Ashland arrived with their 15-year-old daughter, April.

Ashland attempted to calm Charles down, while Abigail maintained her position that Charles must leave.

"What is your contact with Katherine?" asked Ashland.

"Email and text messages," Charles replied.

"I tried to help him. I am done," said Abigail.

Charles felt that both women were against him, and there was one way to escape.

Charles walked to the rear of the property to the barn, finding some weed-eater cord. The lean-to off the side of the barn partially covered a flat-bed trailer. Charles found a roofing rafter 2x4 to wrap the weed-eater cord to and then around his neck.

As Charles made the noose complete, he had forgotten one thing—his phone was still in his pocket. Remembering it, he sent a text message to Abigail, "I am going to end it all now."

Charles would later tell the psychologist he was surprised at how well the noose actually worked at cutting off air to his lungs for a brief time until Abigail found him.

Abigail cried out, "Ashland, please come! Fast!"

Then, "Charles why are you doing this to me?"

Abigail pleaded with Charles as she and Ashland tried to raise his 175 pounds and remove the tight cord from his neck.

Charles's spontaneous decision to leave an apparent hopeless three-way debate with Ashland and Abigail about Katherine and then walk to the barn was a mental miscalculation.

Where do I go and what can fix this problem? Charles had pondered.

On the one hand, Charles found weed eater cord under the lean-to. The eight-foot-tall lean-to covered a one-foot-tall flatbed trailer. The separation between Charles's neck and the trailer was too short for full hanging, as Ashland soon found out when attempting to raise Charles's body enough to free his neck from the cord.

Once freed, Charles pled his guilt and despair with Ashland. Abigail was very upset and resolved to ask Dr. P., the preacher, to come to help.

Dr. P., or "Eddie" as some call him, came over after Charles was escorted inside his home. Ashland was distraught and left with her two children, who had been waiting for her in the family minivan.

April went inside, crying.

The first question Eddie asked Charles was, "Are you drinking tonight?"

The room was quiet. Ashland had left. The preacher would have to say some tough words for Charles to hear. Time was running out for the so-called "family man."

Charles kept his head down as the three sat at the family dinner table. "No drinking. This has nothing to do with alcohol," Charles murmured.

Eddie replied, "Charles, I want you to commit yourself to the psych hospital. What you did tonight is not normal."

Abigail called Charles's boss and told him her husband was not well and would be unable to make the next day's business trip.

Abigail's eldest child, Bradley, had just arrived home. The next day he was to take the CPA exam nearby. Charles would later learn Bradley cried when Abigail told him what was going on.

"Mom, why could Dad not come to his own family when he had this problem?" Bradley asked.

Charles hugged Bradley, then said goodbye ... one of the last hugs he would get from his son for many months to come. Charles was one person Bradley was supposed to be able to rely on, and now that trust was broken. This broke Charles's heart because Donald always taught Charles to be true to the ones that love you and that are supposed to be family.

At the urging of Eddie, Charles entered the psychiatric ward of the local hospital, where he stayed for four days. The waiting room for psych entry was filled with the mentally ill and drug addicts and alcoholics. Each patient received a reclining chair and some water. Charles's first night in the waiting room was long; he spent twenty hours there before being admitted.

It was in the hospital that Charles faced his greatest fear of his life, yet he found hope in a young alcoholic named Ethan, and two other addicts, one dependent on painkillers and the other on hard liquor. The hospital conditions, and those who stayed there, convinced Charles that he needed to make a radical change if he had any chance of regaining the life he once knew.

Charles did not sleep well with two men he did not know. He wrote on a napkin in the psych ward, and later found in his journal impassioned words about his condition.

Charles spent four days in the mental hospital. Abigail called him there to say they would separate. This time his heart did not drop, but he thought, *no way, this is not going to happen. I am an engineer. I can fix this.*

Emotions, convicts, Ethan, alcoholics, drug addicts— Charles was desperate for a solution. This place had shown him a life he did not want.

Rather than feeling sorry for himself, after a sleepless night in a small three-bed room with two alcoholics, Charles awoke at a crossroad. He was either to turn to despair or turn to encouraging others. He chose to get to know the other patients and hopefully say something that would encourage them.

"Crossroad" or "stop sign" were terms given to Charles by the third-shift psychiatrist the night before. While Charles waited to be admitted to the psych ward, he had been interviewed by the hospital psychiatrist. The psychiatrist, an African-American woman in her thirties, told Charles he needed to love life and be thankful.

"Charles, come on back to my office where there is less commotion in the emergency room", the lady directed.

The emergency room was actually the waiting area for mental patients before being admitted to the psych ward.

"Tell me about yourself Charles. Why are you here?"

"I am having an affair. I can't fix it so I tried to manipulate my wife and yes I am desparate for a real solution", Charles pleaded.

"You need to turn down the 'right' road when you come to a stop sign," the doctor urged. "If not, you are going to hate life", she further scolded him.

He was also deeply affected by Abigail's declaration of separation on the phone with him in the hospital.

"May I use the phone to call my wife?" Charles pleaded with the psych ward nurse. "You'll have to wait! You think this is a Holiday Inn!" she scolded Charles.

Among the other two dozen mentally ill patients, many in their 20's, Charles was handed the phone and called Abigail. "I will stop all contact with Katherine and work on myself. Please, we can work this out?", Charles exclaimed to Abigail. "I am sorry but we will separate. You will have to find your own place", Abigail said softly.

Charles knew the length of his stay at the mental hospital was based on his behavior observed by the nurses and psychiatrists.

Dr. Loveblood was assigned to Charles. Unlike most patients Charles was told he was not mentally ill, nor did he have any disorders except anxiety and made poor decisions with his marriage. Charles was diagnosed with anxiety and nothing more. Good news - but the hard work was yet to be done.

The hospital stay by Charles resulted in deep rethinking on his part, orchestrated by some leading psychiatrists and counselors. Charles was profoundly affected by the mental ward patients—he certainly did not want to be there.

Arriving at the ward's breakfast table, the head nurse, an abrupt, tall, wide-shouldered lady, passed out eggs and bread along with some orange juice. Charles looked across the table and saw a young man who was keeping his head down and engaging in no conversation.

Next to Charles was Olivia, a woman in her thirties, who Charles later learned had a master's degree in psychology and was an alcoholic. She had lost her driver's license many times for driving while impaired, and she forfeited a federal job in Washington, DC, for poor performance due to the liquor bottle. Charles thought how can an attractive intelligent woman be a repeat patient in a mental ward of a hospital. "Are you on Linkedin?", Olivia asked Charles. Charles responded, "Yes and I hope to stay in touch with your progress to gain employment again."

Then there was Natalie, who overdosed on pain killers because she was depressed that her attorney ex-husband had dumped her for a younger, more attractive lady.

"What are you here for, Charles?" Natalie asked, her head down, glasses on the end of her nose.

"I am not here for alcohol, drugs, or any medications. I cheated on my wife," Charles asserted quietly.

"You know she wants to take you back; you know that, right?" said Natalie to Charles with a straight face.

One of the first patients he met had been a twenty-one-year-old alcoholic, Ethan.

Ethan and Charles started a conversation one night. They slept on bunk beds, short ones with a patient monitor that would tell the head nurse if a patient got up from the bed. Charles could not sleep. He was sad about his behavior during the last few days and upset by the news Abigail gave him earlier that day about wanting a separation.

Nevertheless, Charles decided to query Ethan about whom he was and why he started drinking alcohol.

"How old are you? Are you really an alcoholic?", Charles asked politely. Ethan was sitting below Charles on the bunk bed.

"Yes, it all started at Thomas Wingate High School. I got involved with drugs in the 10th grade. My parents were split up at the time. I was looking for a role model, a father figure to guide me", Ethan told Charles.

Charles pondered the young man's statement which made him sad and then replied: "I am sorry, Ethan. Have you ever prayed to God to help you through your addiction?"

"If God is big enough to create this universe He can surely help me", Ethan responded.. Ethan went on to tell Charles that he was married, but his wife would not take him back until he became completely sober and clean. Ethan and his wife had a one-year-old son. Toward the end of their conversation, Ethan and Charles discussed the Deity or God.

Charles wrote on a napkin in the small hospital room: "Misery is medicine for my selfish behavior." Then he recalled the lessons from the female psychiatrist:

1. *When I am at a "crossroads" of a decision, between what "feels good" and the "right thing," I must choose the latter. Some of the historical decisions that are critical include choosing between attending social functions and consuming alcoholic beverages, flirting versus being a gentleman, between "cutting corners in business" and being totally honest with vendors and clients. Put my spouse before me.*
2. *Work hard and play hard.*
3. *Do I want to be married? Yes, I do.*
4. *Do I love Abigail? Yes, but I must show it the way she needs to receive it—quality time not just physical pleasures.*

Staring out the hospital window, not knowing whether his wife would ever take him back, he wrote a poem called "Colors in Me:"

Blue Skies
But I am not blue
White Clouds
I can be pure
Red Blood
Gives me Life
Green grass
I lay on a summer day—breath
Yellow flowers, sunflowers
Radiate
Brown Eyes
My mother's genes in me

Black people
Are soulful and so full of soul
Orange(s)
Fruit that keeps me healthy
All colors are
A rainbow- does not end
White light is
All colors and truth
I will not hide the truth

The second day at the psych hospital, Charles decided to make the most of his time. He had no material possessions, as they were not allowed in a psych ward. But the paper sack sent to him by Abigail containing some clothes soon became his art work.

On the paper sack Charles wrote: "Believe in Us" and "Abigail, do not give up on me."

Charles knew he would have the opportunity to give the paper sack artwork to Abigail on his exit. But when would Charles get out? This kept haunting him day after day....

The third day, the counselor asked Charles to write down his goals, which were: 1.) work with an accountability partner, Bobby, daily; 2.) talk to the case manager about his feelings; 3.) discover what are the mental triggers that cause negative emotions; and, finally, 4.) find some "coping mechanisms" when helplessness creeps in.

Charles wrote a letter to Abigail:

Life is short and fleeting. The decision we will make will have an enormous emotional, financial, and spiritual impact on us, our children, family, and friends. I am asking that we sit down with a facilitator such as Eddie (Dr. P.), Bobby, or someone of your choice to seriously discuss the decision (to separate). You may think your mind is made up; however, could it be your hurt and pain masks what is really important? My plan is to live on my own for three weeks, attend therapy, and meet you again on your birthday.

Charles was picked up by Abigail on Sunday at the hospital, four days after his attempted suicide. Charles arrived home to find that Abigail had packed him a crate of clothes, some water bottles, and a magnet sign that read: "Never ever give up."

Charles's desperation to find an answer, to decide between Katherine and Abigail, had been made for him. There would be no more Katherine for him, and all his energy would need to be toward Abigail to have any chance of reconciliation.

But reconciliation was not what Abigail was thinking about. She wanted two things: space and healing. Bobby told Charles he had a "long road ahead of him."

Charles found a Motel 6 for a four week stay. Living with poor folks, the downtrodden, and the unemployed made Charles humble. Humility he found while in the hospital's psych ward.

Charles would not sleep waking up in sweat in the middle of the night, wanting his wife and the comfort he once knew. And asking "Where are you father?"

The only thing he knew was an eternal being who he pleaded to for mercy and wisdom. Mercy for his past sins and wisdom to carry on.

Reading his Bible then leaving the motel at 5:30 a.m., he would meet men from a local church who would share stories and read the Bible together.

During these times of sorrow, he had to rely on divine intervention to get him through sleepless nights, shame, embarrassment, poor work performance, and hopelessness.

When will this marriage be able to thrive again? Charles pondered.

Meanwhile, Charles's teaching performance was masked briefly by his inner challenges to be a better husband and father. Days of temporary depression would set in. In his loneliness, he turned to the Deity.

However, his relationship with Katherine needed closure; she had not corresponded with Charles for several weeks. Before heading to the motel, Charles spent some time at his office working on a deadline for an engineering project. Concentration had been a concern for Charles during his affair with Katherine. She had stolen his heart and the limerence was over-powering his emotions. The hospital stay, Abigail's ultimatum to separate and Psalm 32 had changed Charles. He now would make the best decision of his life.

On March 14, 2017, Katherine showed up at Charles's office, a second-floor room with windows facing the front and side.

At 8:30 p.m., the doorbell rang. Charles was by himself and thought it was odd the doorbell would ring that late at night. The door bell and knocks kept coming from downstairs.

Peeking out the rear seond floor window, he saw Katherine's white Honda Accord and a glimpse of her face; she had a determined, look as she stood by the office door.

"I am not going down to let her in my office. I kind of miss her. She is a friend now? No. This is a 'stop sign' and I will turn in the right direction this time", Charles surmised.

Charles called Bobby to tell him Katherine came by. "Man I am proud of you. You just made the second big step in a long road to recovery!", Bobby said with understanding.

Bobby was proud of Charles, who for once had told the truth and would not respond to Katherine. Not responding to an hour and half of her doorbell rings infuriated Katherine.

Katherine threw candy at Charles's window while he talked to Bobby, his faithful friend. While he and Abigail were separated, Charles was now "working on himself." This meant Abigail could not help him, and so they only talked by phone.

The deep hurt Abigail felt meant that she did not want to see Charles until he was "well."

Katherine camped by his office door, but she could not see Charles. After two hours, she left Charles's parking lot, having had no contact with him.

Charles continued to shun contact with Katherine, although two weeks later he did attempt to call her, then realized he had erased all her information, including her business details, from his phone. A few days later, when Abigail asked if he had had any contact, this time he could say with confidence and honesty—no.

Charles believed in and now practiced the "stop sign" to manage his thoughts, emotions, and behavior. This adherence to a proven psychological practice and his renewed interest in reading about the moral code in the *Bible* propelled Charles toward godly ideals and moral undertakings. He still hoped to reconcile with Abigail.

ABIGAIL

Donald's patriarchic dream was fully alive in 1987 on a warm spring day in Carolina. Charles was a sophomore engineering student at N.C. State University. Abigail was a sophomore at UNC-Greensboro, once called "Women's College."

Donald could not be happier. He and Abigail would ride together in the little white pickup truck some 90 miles to see Charles at N.C. State. Donald adored Abigail, and for good reason. Donald was proud Charles chose to pursue such a lovely woman. And Abigail would only learn later she would carry on Donald's dream after his death.

Abigail admired Donald for several reasons, not just because he was Charles's dad. She was riding with a World War II hero, a kind man, gentle conversationalist, a father figure. His family values were her family values. They both liked good wholesome conversation, sitting around a fireplace in the winter and working in the yard.

Abigail was dressed in jeans and a blue blouse to match her flowing blond hair. Her hazel eyes and slender body were elements of her attractiveness. Abigail was also attractive because of her kindness and the gentle words she spoke.

Along the way to visit Charles, Donald would treat Abigail to visiting an antique book store in Durham and enjoying an ice cream cone. Ice cream was Donald's favorite dessert and most likely contributed to his high blood pressure (aggravated by a lack of exercise). Six months later, Abigail attended to Mary and Donald in the hospital's ICU, where he lay after his massive heart attack, while Charles was in the mountains. But for this spring day, the dream lived on.

Abigail was born in 1967, the middle child of five children. Unlike Charles, she learned how to share with others at an early age. Her home was noisy with family and friends. She and her siblings played kickball almost daily with friends in their lower-middle-class neighborhood. As she and her siblings grew to adulthood, they shared memories, cars, clothes, and their money.

In contrast, Charles grew up by himself. His brother Danny left the home when Charles was thirteen. Charles was never lacking for the basic necessities of life. He liked to work on devices alone and sometimes would ride his bike to the city to play football with friends. He started a manual labor job at the age of twelve: painting, working on a small farm, working on his car, and learning carpentry from Donald.

Abigail had to work for everything she had, fending for herself to buy clothes, to purchase a car and to pay for her college education through a Stafford Loan, while holding down a job working at Greensboro's Yum Yum Ice Cream Shop.

She bought a 1976 Chevrolet Nova from money she made working at Yum Yum and U-Haul.

Again, in contrast, Donald helped Charles buy his first car, a 1977 Mustang, paying all but $175.

When Abigail's siblings hurt each other emotionally, she

learned how to forgive them. When Abigail's siblings quarreled, one would take up for the other. They made up. They cried. They laughed. This unselfish behavior still exists today.

Abigail was a model student in high school and college and well behaved. She made the Beta Club with all-As and was included in the National Honor Society her senior year. She never got into trouble at school. She played by all the rules.

On the other hand, Charles liked sports and playing percussion instruments. He did not get into any serious trouble at school but was mischievous and independent. As a senior in high school, he fell in puppy love with a sophomore and then chased her, before college opened up new relationships.

Rather than focus on relationships with men, Abigail focused her extra time at her church by being on the debate team.

These comparisons reveal some positive characteristics of Abigail while suggesting Charles had less of them. Did the environment in which Abigail grew up shape her moral character, her insistence on "playing by all the rules"? Did Charles's promiscuous behavior derive from the self-centered home he grew up in as a boy, and to a lesser extent from his experiences as a college student?

The nature vs. nurture debate within psychology is concerned with the extent to which particular aspects of behavior are either inherited (i.e., genetic, nature) or acquired (i.e., learned, nurture) characteristics. Did Abigail inherit her unselfish behavior and did Charles's alcoholic grandfather pass down the sins of the grandfather? Charles may never know the answer to these questions, but he finally came to realize his worldly thoughts were that he did not deserve an unselfish, forgiving woman like Abigail.

Certainly, parents do influence their children due to genetic make-up, their teachings, and to a lesser extent their legal hedges (for example, wills and inheritances).

Abigail's parents were family centered. Seven people shared

time and space in a modest four-bedroom home. Through Abigail's interactions with her four siblings and devoted parents, she learned to distinguish good from bad and right from wrong. This shaped who she was and who she would become.

Although her genes laid out a blueprint for Abigail's potential development, they did not fully determine who she became. Instead, her environment in a close-knit family created by her parents presented an atmosphere that helped instruct and direct her genes. Some psychologists would assert good parents are only "gene therapists," but others would argue for the importance of the family environment.

Abigail received no special treatment from her parents, no flashcards, no tutors and no phone calls to teachers asking for help or explanation on performance scores. Charles's mother, on the other hand, arranged for tutors and interacted with teachers, attempting to give Charles perhaps more than he deserved. Abigail was independent, hard-working, unselfish, dedicated ... not just morally inclined, but truly God-fearing.

Donald and Mary considered Abigail to be an angel sent to Charles, and they treated her like one of their own children, a daughter they loved (in fact, Deborah was jealous of Abigail).

It was Abigail who left anonymous letters on Charles's windshield during the summer of 1986 while he was a substitute teacher at the local elementary school. Abigail was working at the nearby U-Haul; each day before work she would stop by Charles's car.

Charles thought the letters, hand-written on the old handwriting rule books, were left on his car by one of the fifth-grade girls. He was wrong.

One of those letters read:

Dear Mr. Spencer,

I enjoy you as a substitute teacher. You make class fun for learning. Thank you again.

Sincerely,
Elizabeth

Abigail later confessed she wrote all the letters, thirty in all, for thirty days in a row.

Charles would eventually enjoy writing, but early in their courtship, it was Abigail who would take time to write Charles.

Abigail graduated in May of 1989 from the University of North Carolina at Chapel Hill and married Charles three months later.

Later, after twenty-six years of marriage, Abigail wrote:

Dear Charles Spencer,

Twenty-five years ago, I became your wife.

We both were young but made a commitment to have a godly marriage together. We have been blessed through the trials and challenges of marriage. I am truly thankful for you and our children.

As we start our twenty-sixth year together, I want you to know in front of our family and friends, I promise to continue to love you, respect you, comfort you and pray for you, forsake all others and remain faithful to you in sickness and health 'til death do us part.

I am your helpmate and friend. I have an endless love for you and pray God will bless us with many more years together.

Love,
Abigail

Her business colleagues have stated she "plays by all the rules" and never utters a harsh word for anyone. Unlike the majority of Christian and non-Christian woman, Abigail never spread one rumor in her entire life.

When Charles's anger would be fueled by those who wanted to harm him, Abigail would respond, "You cannot control that issue; you have done all you can—give it to God."

In any proper definition of a moral, godly woman, Abigail would fit the description.

A GODLY WOMAN, A GODLY WIFE

A godly woman has the opportunity to be one of the greatest influencers on earth. The striking beauty of her spirit may win the soul of her unbelieving husband or in this case, the husband, Charles, who strayed, manipulated, was confused, and became desperate to solve a crisis that was not solvable by man's laws or rules.

Historically, straying and adultery were punishable by death in the first century, by mutilation in the Middle Ages, and still are illegal acts today in some countries. Perhaps this is what Charles and other code breakers need today to send a message that adultery and other sinful acts need to be punished. But the pain Charles would feel from breaking the moral code would eventually bring about a punishment rooted in forgiveness and a deep abiding love.

Abigail's adherence to God's design in marriage proclaimed what Jesus said to the religious law-keepers in Matthew 19:4–6:

> The pious leaders tried to trap Him in a debate about the Law: "Does the Law say a man can divorce his wife for any reason?"
>
> Jesus said to them, "Have you not read that He who made them in the first place made them man and woman? It says, 'For this reason a man will leave his father and his mother and will live with his wife. The two will become one.' So they are no longer two but one. Let no man divide what God has put together."

Abigail's faith in, and knowledge of, God and the *Bible* she had learned as a teenage girl spilled over into her sphere of ministry—her family and her few close friends. What an example of a Godly woman: to forgive a man who caused her so much pain! She would soon forgive her husband—not because of what he did, not for his counseling sessions, nor his renewed vigor for the moral code, but solely for the example of Jesus.

Abigail's beliefs and her devotion are similar to Sarah in the *Bible*. In Old Testament times, the Jewish holy women who hoped in God would dress themselves appropriately and submit to their husbands, as Sarah obeyed Abraham, calling him "Lord." Charles did not expect this from Abigail because he had not fully studied the meaning of submission in a Christian marriage.

For a Christian woman like Abigail, her rest in God is partly the submission to her husband. Charles did not realize how blessed he was to have a woman like Abigail.

In the *Bible*, Sarah submitted to Abraham because she trusted in and obeyed God. Her submission to her husband was not due to her reliance upon Abraham. Rather, her eyes were fixed on a trustworthy God who was worthy of her submission.

Charles wondered, after all his shortcomings including adultery and lack of love for her, why did she still submit to him? After all, Abigail's complaint to Charles was that she was tired of submitting to someone who defiled the marriage bed.

During the marital strife and family crisis, while Charles' heart was with another one, Abigail got on her hands and knees and prayed for days and hours for healing. Despite being wounded by Charles, she prayed for him daily, hourly, minute by minute at home and at work. Her work colleagues thought she should not take Charles back, the typical response from the a secular society with more than fifty percent divorce rate.

Abigail's parents, her devotion to God, and family helped shape her response to an unfaithful spouse.

A encounter with her God came the night Charles was with

Katherine at Rainbow's End. Abigail called her best friend Eve desperate she covet prayers for her marriage and Charles to turn from evil. On December 4, 2016, in the middle of the night, Abigail prayed for six hours. With tears of sorrow pouring from her face, she called Charles on the phone. Charles was sleeping with Katherine and stumbled to answer the phone. In tears Abigail said, "Charles, I am praying for you and God is with me; I will let you go." Then Abigail heard a special song came on the radio. Her journal of 5 December 2016 records the following lyrics from the singer Kari Jobe [used here with permission]:

When I walk through deep waters,
I know that You will be with me.
When I'm standing in the fire,
I will not be overcome.
Through the valley of the shadow
I will not fear.
I am not alone.
I am not alone.
You will go before me.
You will never leave me.
I am not alone.
I am not alone.
You will go before me.
You will never leave me.

In the midst of deep sorrow,
I see Your light is breaking through.
The dark of night will not overtake me
I am pressing into You.
Lord, You fight my every battle.
Oh, and I will not fear.
I am not alone.
I am not alone

You will go before me.
You will never leave me.

You amaze me,
You call me as Your own.

You're my strength.
You're my defender.
You're my refuge in the storm.
Through these trials.
You've always been faithful.
You bring healing to my soul.
I am not alone.
You will never leave me.

Charles would later learn the deep, abiding love of his wife, Abigail, a love he himself did not possess. As Charles would tell his closest friend, Bobby, after marriage reconciliation in August of 2017, "I do not deserve this woman; she is a godly woman. She is the real deal."

Charles wrote this poem while contemplating the woman Abigail:

The eyes of this woman
Are not the eyes of this man.
Her eyes are radiant, a greenish blue and true.
The hands of this woman
Are not the hands of this man.
Her hands are precise,
Straight, measuring and effective.
The heart of this woman
Is bigger than the heart of this man.
Her heart is vibrant, forgiving, and caring.
The mind of this woman
Thinks before it speaks,
The work of this woman
Starts early to ready her day,

Is better than the labor of this man.
What then is left of this woman?
A little girl riding her bike and asking, "What kind of woman will I be?"
And answers—"This woman,
This man can't be, or ever be,
As great as she is for we."

Charles would also learn in the next year that Abigail's love language was quality time and words of affirmation, not physical touch or deeds.

Abigail shared a letter she wrote to Charles during the last week of Donald's life while he took his last breath in intensive care:

> I have thought about your daddy a lot. He is a good man of God and I remember the scripture *Luke 9*:56 "For the Son of man is not come to destroy (men's lives) but to save them." I know your daddy will be in heaven when God takes him home. I am so thankful for the times I shared with Donald Spencer. He has influenced my life by his good qualities. You are caring, loving, friendly, hard-working and quiet, just as your father is. I just want you to lock it in your head that I will never leave you for anyone else or when things get tough, either.... All my love, Abigail.

RECONCILIATION

Dr. P, also known as Eddie, called Dr. B. a month earlier and recommended that Charles see Dr. B a prominent Christo-centric family counselor. "Dr. B – I have a friend who is in some serious problems with his family. He needs to see a counselor immediately", Eddie announced on the phone with Charles sitting quietly in his church office.

Abigail had been seeing Dr. B. after the crisis to obtain advice about how to heal her broken heart. The metaphor Dr. B.

used was the human heart, which after an attack or damage or surgery, needs several types of doctors, as well as friends and counselors, to help it heal.

Abigail started a program of healing, through the guidance of Dr. B. She specifically wanted to see Dr. B., being comfortable with his Christo-centric philosophy, based on the examples found in the *Bible* and the healing power of Jesus Christ.

Abigail started seeing Dr. B. regularly, but when Charles attempted suicide the second time, she almost gave up until Ashland's prodding of her. "I know you are in a lot of pain and I would run from Charles, but you need Dr. B's counseling. You can not do it alone", Ashland told Abigail.

In tears, Abigail would maintain her deep commitment to the Deity and the ten commandments and exhort to Ashland: "I still love him, but he is not the man he was just six months ago- something drastic has to change". Then, one day at the urging of Ashland, over a tearful conversation, she diverted her vehicle to go to see Dr. B. in lieu of stopping at the grocery store.

At this point, Abigail agreed to try counseling one more time. It was March of 2017.

What would Charles's mother, Mary, have thought?

Once, Mary had urged Charles, in the second year of his marriage, "Don't you ever leave Abigail."

Charles knew Mary would say this; after all, her father, the alcoholic, was not a good father and was not around to support his wife.

Donald's dream of how a family should behave had become Mary's mission to pass on to her children. What Charles was doing to his family was to shatter that dream, but not for long....

The key components of a marriage are passion, commitment, and intimacy.

Eventually, Abigail forgave Charles and invited him back into their family. Charles asked Abigail why she forgave him.

She responded, "It was nothing you did. I forgave you be-cause of a deep conviction I have in my heart and soul about the love of God. In my deepest moments that December third night, while you slept with Katherine, I got on my hands and knees and prayed for six hours. My friend E. prayed with me on the phone. It is because of my deep faith in God, I forgave you, not because of who you are or what you did. I am giving you a gift you do not deserve, much like God gave to me in his son Jesus Christ. Jesus' death was the price paid for the sins of man; for my sins, he died a horrific death on a tree, and I did not deserve his gift".

Charles recorded in his journal:

Dear Abigail,

Perhaps you may doubt my repentance, my emotional tur-moil, and now my seeking for peace and to know God. I am on a spiritual journey that most in the "world" would not believe after my immoral behavior, but the only thing that matters is we give God the credit for our marriage recon-ciliation and individual growth.

Then God reminded me today these words I penned: "The hand of God was on me, for in my youth the Lord God saved me."

No more backsliding for me.

Then today the Lord reminded me in my quiet time about David of the *Bible*, the teenager who defeated a big man. David's psalms demonstrate he was a man after God's heart, yet in his laziness he committed adultery and in his anger killed Uriah, his own soldier.

These psalms are how I changed that Pearl Harbor Day in December of 2016, when my bones were dying and my mind moaning, when the stillness of our quiet home met your wedding picture in my hands and simultaneously a Divine intervention:

Psalm 32 [New International Version]

Blessed is the one whose transgressions are forgiven, whose sins are covered. Blessed is the one whose sin the LORD does not count against them and in whose spirit is no deceit. When I kept silent, my bones wasted away through my groaning all day long. For day and night your hand was heavy on me; my strength was sapped as in the heat of summer. Then I acknowledged my sin to you and did not cover up my iniquity. I said, "I will confess my transgressions to the LORD." And you forgave the guilt of my sin. Therefore, let all the faithful pray to you while you may be found; surely the rising of the mighty waters will not reach them. You are my hiding place; you will protect me from trouble and surround me with songs of deliverance. I will instruct you and teach you in the way you should go; I will counsel you with my loving eye on you. Do not be like the horse or the mule, which have no understanding but must be controlled by bit and bridle or they will not come to you. Many are the woes of the wicked, but the LORD's unfailing love surrounds the one who trusts in him. Rejoice in the LORD and be glad, you righteous; sing, all you who are upright in heart!"

CHAPTER 15

THE MIRACLE—MARRIAGE RESTORATION IN ONE YEAR

"Do miracles really happen?" Charles pondered and prayed for daily, if not hourly. "Will it take a miracle to restore this marriage?" Charles thought. "My father died young and no miracle occured. My siblings do not talk to me. Danny and his attorneys are unethical. Can a miracle restore all these broken relationships?" Charles told himself over and over.

Miracles have existed in history and two-thirds of Americans believe in them according to a 2016 Barna poll. But two-thirds of Americans do not believe in marriage restoration and breaking marital moral code is frowned upon by the majority of Americans

Miracles are demonstrated in spiritual forces and in the *Bible*. Modern-day people claim they were healed or had near-death experiences through a miracle. Essentially, a miracle is an unusual manifestation of God's power designed to accomplish a specific purpose. The consistent Christian recognizes that God's power is constantly displayed in the clockwork operation of the universe, perhaps a continuous miracle.

Most definitions given for the word "miracle" are not complete. The popular Christian author and broadcaster, former atheist C.S. Lewis, wrote this in the introduction to one of his books: "I use the word miracle to mean an interference with Nature by supernatural power."

To save the marriage of Charles and Abigail, a supernatural power would be needed to heal her heart and change Charles's mind and soul. Something supernatural beyond casual language, self-help books or psychological counseling would be required to save the marriage from Charles' deep hole he dug and Abigail's painful scars.

Although knowledge obtained and behavioral changes by Charles would be important, it was not the critical remedy or the healer. Charles recorded several entries and wise quotes in his journal during the weekly visits with Abigail and Dr. B. Below are some of them:

Restoring intimacy and trust in a damaged relationship was the first topic Dr. B. introduced. He then stated that painful surprises, betrayals, unfaithfulness, lack of full disclosure, lying, cover-ups, stubbornness, and inability to make amends become part of the damage assessment.

The following items explain destruction of trust and the re-building of trust—depending on how Charles, would do it:

1. Stop hurting each other.

2. Put your partner's needs and wishes ahead of your own—betrayal always involves putting one's own needs and wishes ahead of the other partner. That partner quickly learns to not trust the one who keeps on hurting them.

3. Make full disclosure—trust losses occur when information is withheld, when troubling secrets are discovered. Painful surprises can destroy a relationship faster than anything.

4. Walk faithfully with God—if a spouse believes in God and then follows the precepts of the Deity, s/he is unlikely to break the moral code, at least the probability of success in code adherence increases with more knowledge of the laws of God.

5. Apologize and ask for forgiveness from God, if you make a major mistake.

Furthermore, communication is at the heart of everything. It builds relationships, and it destroys them. No matter how much Abigail or Charles tried to avoid effective communication, it is impossible to do so and succeed in marriage. Whether a person, especially in a marriage relationship, is speaking or silent, they are communicating. But even with much practice, effective communication isn't easy.

To Charles's surprise, Abigail revealed the pain caused by his miscommunication for fifteen years, which still resonated in her heart. Dr. B. explained this is why it's important to develop excellent communication skills. Healthy, mature communication is the revelation of your true self to someone/something that is divine and perfect, God.

"You do not know me," Abigail told Charles over and over during their restoration efforts. Charles knew it was true. He had spent twenty-plus years focusing on career, money, fitness, and hobbies, giving the leftovers to Abigail.

What looked like a good marriage was masked by surface talk and secrets. Patriarch Donald's dream for a happy, close family had been passed to Mary, and Mary thought Charles was different, that his family was special.

Dr. B. then quoted a verse from the *Bible:* "Do not let any unwholesome talk come out of your mouths, but only what is helpful for building others up according to their needs, that it may benefit those who listen." (Ephesians 4:29)

The three essential ingredients in a relationship are passion, intimacy, and commitment.

Developing intimacy is crucial: intimacy is *not* sex. Passion is *not* sex. Commitment is required.

Charles continued to write in his journal things he learned from participating in the counseling session with Abigail and Dr. B.:

> "One of the most important tasks to be accomplished in a marriage is to develop a list of mutually acceptable expectations," Dr. B. explained. Dr. B. also said most marital problems are because of unmet expectations.

Abigail confided that she thought Charles had a hidden agenda when they were alone or starting to be romantic: "Do you really plan our sex, and do you want more than just talking and holding hands?"

"Abigail, you need to tell me what you want. I like being romantic and holding hands and sharing deep thoughts," Charles tried to explain.

In the end, Donald's dream was shattered, but not by Abigail. She played by all the rules, remained faithful to her maker and her husband. On the other hand, Donald's children each broke some rule, law, or ethical ordinance:

> Deborah's prolonged marriage appears to be without major difficulties and by all accounts is succeeding. But Deborah's laziness in not seeking the truth in her siblings demonstrates her failure to live up to Donald's dream for family involvement and harmony.

> Charles created an unstable marriage for about six months, but it has been reconciled and may be stronger than ever before.

> How about Danny? He and his wife, Martha, had a rocky marriage, and they split up after twenty-six years. Unlike Charles, who became humble and contrite for his immoral behavior, Danny would not reconcile with his spouse; only time will tell if he will be a lonely man one day.

EPILOGUE

LESSONS LEARNED

By now, you, the reader, realize that this "novel" is based closely on real life, with some changes made to preserve privacy and others done to allow realistic details, like conversations, to be presented, though they are only approximations of what actually happened.

I have written this story as a vehicle to transmit what I considered important principles, in estate business, family and marriages. I will expand on these in what follows.

MARRIAGE

Despite Charles's ethical behavior in most all accounts in his profession, at work and at home, he carried a secret that broke the moral code, one in which he dreamed of a time to ask his father Donald, "What do I do, Dad?"

"Do you really understand the original purpose for marriage?", Abigail questioned Charles.

"It is a vow and it keeps an orderly society" responded Charles.

"No! Marriage is a sacred covenant between one man and one woman. The two become one, one flesh!" Abigail scolded

Charles as her tears started to fall.

Charles' secret was that he was struggling with an extra-marital relationship that would almost drown him in a sea-like abyss.

The children of Donald would not carry on the dream and his legacy.

But there is a victory to the story.

Charles had been married twenty-seven years to a devoted wife and mother. Even after three children, Abigail remained an attractive lady. Abigail's excellent qualities make the marital conflict caused by Charles even more perplexing. So why did Charles stray, and why do men who have loving wives stray? Despite the tendency to offer a simple reason like selfishness, there are other motives.

Charles created a painful emotional crisis for his family and endured a spiritual conflict that almost destroyed the life he knew. What kind of man would do that? Why did he do that?

The experiences in this book are written to inspire others who may be going through a painful family or marriage crisis. Some thoughts that led up to the affair were a desire to converse with those of the opposite sex while under the influence of alcohol. Charles's drinking alcohol and flirting did not cause the straying; he chose to break the moral code, but drinking did lower inhibitions and make flirting easier.

Playboy Magazine and erotic images on the Internet distort one's thoughts, unfairly comparing the wife to some erotic person or fantasy.

Below are some of the instructional activities that helped Charles and his family in marriage restoration:

The past cannot be changed, and the future is uncertain. As clichéd as it sounds, you are not guaranteed tomorrow. There is no guarantee your health will be good nor that your spouse will love you the next day.

Only today can be changed. So, what was the change needed to reconcile and then restore a broken marriage, a marriage that had appeared to be pure, respectful, and loving? It was a marriage like a machine, moving along, producing babies, generating economic value, and even yielding times of passion and commitment.

Strategies can help. What brought Abigail and Charles from a seemingly hopeless situation he created to a marriage that is vibrant and solid? For this married couple, some of the strategies that made a major difference included:

- **Focus on changing yourself**

As time passed, Charles was focused on career, running and training for a marathon, and traveling. His ego was unchecked. Soon after his Japan experience in 2004, his ego exploded as another woman filled up his cup with song and dance, a cup properly reserved for his wife.

The percentage of U.S. married men that cheat is twenty-two percent, according to one source [http://www.divorcestatistics.info/latest-infidelity-statistics-of-usa.html]. The same source indicates fourteen percent of women have done so. Men are found to cheat primarily for sex, women primarily for emotional connection.

These stats most likely underestimate cheating, especially by men, since rates of divorce and affairs, and the availability of pornography, are all increasing. After all, few men will admit to cheating or to viewing pornography.

Men rarely seek counseling for their struggles with the moral code or unethical practices. Why? Pride, ego and concern about their image hinders counseling. Men become complacent in their personal growth.

Take former Senator John Edwards, for example; he told the truth only after he was caught cheating. Was he sorrowful because he got busted or was it true godly sorrow? Did he refrain from telling the truth to protect his image and his career?

A research study of the effects of viewing pornographic images found a strong correlation to a romantic breakup later on in the marriage [https://www.psychologytoday.com/blog/experimentations/201707/pornography-and-broken-relationships].

This makes logical sense because viewing pornography is like one partner psychologically having an affair with a secret fantasy person. Then only part of the emotional energy is spent toward the spouse. Unless one hundred percent of energy is directed toward the spouse, the marriage will start to decay.

The wife of great actor Denzel Washington, married thirty-five years, said there was no secret to their longevity as a couple: "Our faith," she shared. "Nothing is magic, it's just work."

Denzel added, "I got a good woman—that's the first thing. You just keep working at it."

Marriages will go stale and complacent without lots of work, and not the work men and women go to in business; rather, what's required is quality time together—talking, walking, and getting to know their inner selves.

Keeping a secret from your spouse about another person, whether real or fantasy, is not a good idea, just as unwise as hiding your money and spending habits. Both will destroy trust. One may be addictive. Jesus Christ said, in *Matthew* 5:28, "But I tell you that anyone who looks at a woman lustfully has already committed adultery with her in his heart."

During their crisis of 2016–2017, Charles realized he needed to change. The affair was not Abigail's fault. She was still an attractive woman, and the two were still having and enjoying sex. So, why was Charles unfulfilled? Selfishness or ego alone is not a valid reason.

Charles began to consider ways that he could change (rather than waiting for Abigail to change). How could Charles respond to her differently—with more kindness and patience and humility?

How could Charles respond to stress, to constantly feeling overwhelmed, with more calmness and perhaps more humor? Charles decided that he would work on himself, without expecting change in return (at least, not right away). Charles stopped casual drinking, not because alcohol is "bad," but because these beverages hindered his relationship with Abigail and the Deity. Charles also would implement the "stop sign" mental routine.

If Charles came to a "crossroads," where alcohol was on the left and another sexy woman on the right, he was to stop, think, and go straight instead of turning. "Turning the wrong way may cost you your life," the emergency room psychiatrist told Charles during the crisis peak.

When you're faced with a near-death crisis, literally, emotionally, and spiritually, there is hope. During a crisis, you should seek the help of trained counselors, but do not tell your story to just anyone. Confide in those who, despite your immorality, would only judge you after judging themselves.

What did Jesus say about judging others? Whether you are a Christian or just believe Jesus was simply a good teacher or a prophet of Jewish heritage, you will find valuable what He said in the *Bible, Matthew 7*, about judging others:

Why do you look at the speck of sawdust in your brother's eye and pay no attention to the plank in your own eye? How can you say to your brother, "Let me take the speck out of your eye," when all the time there is a plank in your own eye? You hypocrite, first take the plank out of your own eye, and then you will see clearly to remove the speck from your brother's eye.

• **Acts of kindness**

Some Christian churches, and Christians themselves, have failed to listen, teach, answer, and love according to the main precept in the *Bible*—God's story of salvation. The example of Jesus's love for humanity is the arguably the greatest story ever told. However, saying Jesus was kind is an understatement, but His is a behavior worth modeling.

When a crisis erupts in your life, being kind is unlikely going to be on the top of your to-do list. For Charles, his childhood selfishness would be overcome as a man with deep introspection and conviction on his lack of kindness toward Abigail.

Charles knew that the "little things" in his marriage mattered, but he was considering only the big things—paying the mortgage, completing his education, and paying for three kids' college educations. However, "little things," both positive and negative, matter a lot in a marriage relationship.

So, if lots of little negative things left the marriage in rough shape, he slowly began to seek ways to show small acts of kindness to Abigail. Charles tried to keep doing this even when there was little to no response.

One day Abigail told Charles what she wanted from him: "quality time." This meant he needed to turn off the cell phone, put it in a drawer and be with the woman who bore his three children, who stayed with him when he strayed, whose pain exceeded more than childbirth in knowing her man was with another woman.

- **Knowledge is power**

Knowledge is power, but not the kind of power you may be thinking of. Knowledge is the beginning of wisdom. Wisdom is critical to facing contemptuous life struggles especially marital challenges. Some books and resources that helped Charles during his quest to change included the *Bible* and *The Five Love Languages*, by Gary Chapman. You may think the *Bible* is just another important book written by wise men or you may feel it is outdated and not practical in such advanced technological world.

Before the crisis Charles had thought to himself: "After all my scientific research, I am not 100% certain I believe the creation story. Is it probable, but did we did just evolve and the Bible is a book of myths and tales"?

On the contrary, reading the Bible is not just therapeutic for life, it is a wonderful story of creation culminating with the story of a savior for the world. Jesus lived and the disciples' story is based on historical evidence that demands a verdict.

While chasing career goals and paying those bills, Charles made little time to read so-called "self-help books." However, in changing himself, he completed reading four books of the *Bible*, read Dr. Chapman's book, and attended over twenty-five marriage and family counseling sessions with Dr. B. and Dr. M.

Charles worked on himself and he thought: *it was the end of "ME."* "ME" he would turn upside down to "WE." "WE" meant more time thinking about Abigail and his three children, two of whom who were already grown adults. "ME" needed a radical change.

Charles learned successful marriages, marriages of excellence, require lots of work and lots of energy added by each partner to thrive. Like an apple, a marriage will rot if you do not tend it carefully. You can't leave an apple out in the sun and you can't leave your marriage unattended, or it will become complacent and perhaps wither away.

The counseling sessions revealed Charles knew only part of what makes a woman tick and what she thinks about. Charles learned so much about the fundamental differences in how we are wired as men and women. He found information he had been seeking on respect and what it means to men. Charles learned that most women would rather talk and hold hands than jump into bed for sex.

Sex, Charles learned, should not be equated with love. Love is not sex.

Finally, in knowledge, Charles learned he was not a very good communicator. He talked fluently, but he did not listen enough. There is a scientific reason for two ears and one mouth. In order to detect sounds from all angles, two separated eardrums enable location of sounds.

The *Bible* enjoins us to be "Slow to speak and quick to listen."

Effective communication is the highway on which love can travel.

In Charles's opinion, listening is one of the most powerful tools human beings have because it is the way to learn and grow. Some of you may be saying "But learning is down on my own priorities—I am a self-made man." But to learn your art or your skill or your craft, you have to stop and listen. Even more important is listening to your marriage partner.

- **Focus on the good that can come from pain**

Dr. M. also told Charles that positive changes can come about from very difficult situations. Deep down, Charles believed that somehow, something good would ultimately come out of an intensely painful situation. But Charles caused it. Shame and grief were trying to overtake his positive emotions.

When Charles was a young teenager playing sports, one of his coaches told him, "No pain, no gain." What Charles learned about personal growth from the psychologist Dr. M. was you cannot grow when you are comfortable and complacent. You can only grow when you are "at the edge of a cliff." Will you jump over the valley of despair or stay in it?

- **Exercise**

Another important activity that can help you in crises is exercise. In addition to walking, Abigail and Charles started running. This was a blessing because Charles had been a runner since high school. Abigail rode her bike for some years, but she was never a long-distance runner. Running is like many things in life which initially seem boring and hard.

However, with discipline and a positive psychological outlook, exercise can return both physical and mental benefits.

- **Belief in God**

Finally, some of you reading this book may not believe in God. Some of you believe in a god but not the God of Jesus Christ. Would it be fair to say every man and woman should ask and research the most important questions? *Is there a God? Who created the universe? After coming to a conclusion on God, then who was this Jesus Christ?* The teachings of Jesus Christ include obedience, compassion, and mercy. Jesus showed compassion for all and helped them: the poor, the despised, the outcasts, and wants us to do the same (Matthew 4:24–25; 9:9–13).

During an emotional crisis or personal struggle with addictions, whether alcohol, drugs, sex or psychological deviances, stories of men and woman changing their lives by way of religion, a belief in God, are paramount in the history of civilization. After all, even the Apostle Paul killed church-goers, and yet he will go down in history as one of the most influential followers of Jesus Christ, preaching salvation through trust in Christ.

So how do you know your spouse or mate has really changed after a marital crisis? Time and behavior ... mostly behavior. You have to have deep, godly sorrow for wrong actions and behaviors. Godly sorrow requires the element of repentance, not just contrite words said or written on paper.

You will know your spouse has changed for the better and for good, if he or she does not repeat the negative things once said or done, over days, then months, and then years. There will be displayed a contrite spirit and humility. Consistent behavior is also proof a person changed.

Many men fail in life, but only a few are truly sorry for their actions and turn back for good to the moral code never to be broken again.

• Humility

Humility is a mindset that as soon as you think you are humble you are then not humble. It takes only a little pride and ego to destroy humility really fast: "Pride comes before the fall."

Humility and kindness were two personal traits Charles

needed to work really hard on to be a better man and husband. Charles had learned in management class that being nice in an organization produced better economic results and built teamwork. Charles's problem was he knew this principle academically, but did not put it into practice. Theory and practice are different, and often it is practice that produces actual results, not theory.

As a Ph.D., Charles used the scientific method in lab experiments to learn about the nature of light. However, as a practicing engineer, he found from this life experience that real-world solutions make a difference in folks' lives. Some practical behaviors that help a marriage grow include being humble and kind.

Humility is summed up in Tim McGraw's song "Humble and Kind." In the song, Mr. McGraw asserts that although things may be going well for you, you can lose what you have in a moment. So no matter what your status is in society, meekness is virtuous not wicked or evil.

Tim McGraw also said do not forget those that care about you. "Don't forget the key's under the mat... and the light that glows by the door".

Mr. McGraw emphasizes the traditional and outdated activates in life like going to church, opening the car door for your wife, and visiting Grandpa every chance that you can, "It won't be wasted time. Always stay humble and kind."

And love, Tim McGraw says you should never take for granted: "When you get where you're going, don't forget turn back around, and help the next one in line, always stay humble and kind."

Do dreams come true? Mr McGraw might say when dreams come true and don't come true as in *Shattered Dreams*, always stay humble and kind. He goes on to state when dreams come to you and when the work you put in is understood, let yourself feel the pride, "but always stay humble and kind".

But a change from cruelty and arrogance to kindness and humility does not stop with only these behaviors. During deep emotional pain, a greater power worked for this marriage and that was calling out to the God of the universe through prayer.

Charles did not pray because prayer was obligatory. He prayed because he needed Divine intervention for changing a behavior he could not change by himself. The doctors were only part of the solution.

His wife's heart was barely beating; her heart was broken, and many physicians and doctors were needed to stop the bleeding. In the end, it was the Great Physician who would heal the marriage, and heal each other.

Prayers—the wife's prayers, prayers from true friends and the prayers of many other people for the family—were incredibly powerful. People prayed when the couple had no knowledge of their intercession.

Charles prayed for his wife daily to give him one more chance, for grace and peace and strength daily. He knew that he needed to trust in God, even though the situation felt hopeless. Somehow, amidst the tears and sleepless nights and feeling of numbness, he also experienced an amazing calm during those days while sleeping in a hotel room—truly amazing grace. So, fail and fail big, but do not take chances with your family, your wife or those that love you. The risk you take with these may just cost your life.

FAMILY VALUES

Donald's dream for family was spoiled by hidden agendas and greed in the baby boomers Deborah, Charles, and Danny. Their relationships with each other and among family were superficial.

Donald would be displeased with Danny's manipulative behavior of Mary, masked in "good deeds." Charles broke the dream by being unfaithful to his wife, yet their marriage will survive and thrive more strongly due to the deep, abiding love of Abigail and by Divine intervention.

A strong marriage is something the aging Danny may long for but may have difficulty in finding; it appears he can not remedy deep emotional pain resulting in bitterness and other negative behaviors most moral women would not tolerate.

Danny does not trust people and fears his family is out to take something from him; he would be better off choosing to share what patriarch Donald created for all of them.

Like the Grinch who stole Christmas, who had a small heart, Danny's heart may be hard, as he is confusing shrewd business tactics that enable "success" with family values that leave a legacy for children and generations.

What is the standard by which one defines "family values"? For Donald, his standard was putting his family above his own needs and individual goals. He learned this and the importance of sacrifice on the battle fields of France and Germany in WWII.

A good Christian family is supposed to line up with biblical principles, where each member understands and fulfills a God-given role. The family is not an institution designed by man; the Judeo-Christian concept is that marriage was created by God for the benefit of man, and man has been given stewardship over it.

The basic biblical family unit is composed of one man and one woman, his spouse, and their offspring. The extended family can include relatives by blood or marriage, such as grandparents, nieces, nephews, cousins, aunts, and uncles.

One of the primary principles of the family unit is that it involves a *commitment* ordained by God for the lifetime of the members. The husband and wife are responsible for holding it together, despite any counter-cultural influences. Although divorce is sought and granted much too easily in our society, the *Bible* tells us that God hates divorce.

Swearing "...'til death do us part" does *not* exclude infidelity; the partners must exclude it.

Key principles

Some key principles that apply to all families, even those who may practice other religions, are inclusion and selflessness.

Inclusion—Inclusion almost always requires the family to accept one another and care for each other. Although a little spirited competition can be good, it should never divide the siblings or parents.

For inclusion, here is a question to ask: Do conversations with the spouse include statements of understanding, compassion, and empathy for those who are different or even who may challenge the other person? Whether Charles believed his children were watching or listening to him, the perceptions he and Abigail gave were internalized by the children and become part of the family's culture.

Selflessness—Selflessness is hard but necessary in a family. Selflessness is an important ingredient to marriage, friendships, and relationships. It is also an essential key to happiness and fulfillment. But unfortunately, it is often overlooked. For many years, which led up to the estate crisis and marital strife, Charles did not stop to think how selfish he was. After all, he got up every day for thirty years and went to work, paid the mortgage, the college tuition bills, and took out the trash. Was he really selfish? The answer is yes, thrice over.

Selflessness is often overlooked as a key to happiness because, on the surface, it appears to run contrary to the very notion of being happy. After all, is not the pursuit of happiness selfish? No, it is not. Or at least, it need not be.

Danny is a control freak and likes to possess control over people. Likewise, Charles was not understanding with his wife, Abigail. Deborah wanted to avoid conflict, thinking the estate and family crises could be swept under the rug. Selflessness means you should face your family with the issues that have long-term effects.

Speaking of love, it is a choice; it is not controlling the other person, as indicated by this quotation:

"If your love is only a will to possess, it's not love." —Thích Nhất Hạnh

ISSUES IN FAMILY, ESTATE, AND WILLS

Among the lessons learned are some related to wills and inheritances.

Mary did not have a formal, legally binding will until she had terminal cancer. Her thoughts, as a woman in her eighties, were that she would keep living and would get to the will some other day. A few months before she died, she was escorted by Danny to his long time drinking buddy Mr. Jacky to update her will. After the meeting Mary told Abigail that Danny and Jacky discussed the meeting in a phone conversation breaking the ethical code of attorney-client privilege. There was no discussion with her family and one child directed the process. This harms trust.

As people get older, decisions about topics such as health and retirement tend to become a bit more challenging. So why wait to create or update your will?

The tough decisions we make later in life are often important. They can impact our lives and those of others substantially, meaning there may be fewer opportunities, less time, to recover from any bad decisions we make.

Every man and woman should have a will by fifty years old. Fifty years old is somewhat arbitrary, but a good time to start planning. Do not wait until your health is deteriorating, because by then your ability to make logical decisions may be diminished. On the other hand, things may happen after you have made your will that require modifying it; do so with caution.

So, what generally goes into making a good decision? First, information must be compiled. For a will, if a child is to be executor, which child is trustworthy to be the executor? Which child is mentally stable and has the skills to carry out your desires and wishes?

If there are multiple children involved, then it may be wise to use estate funds and hire an unbiased estate attorney.

Decision-making typically involves identifying goals and then selecting the option most likely to meet them. Think through the available options and compare all of the pros and cons. This requires significant cognitive effort.

Get your emotions under control. Research shows that decision-makers who are able to avoid dwelling on things that have gone wrong in the past will make better decisions about when to walk away from a loss.

Charles was taught the theory of managing emotions, but it is the practice of making good decisions that trumps emotional theory. When deep-rooted negative emotions go unchecked or are not studied by the holder of these emotions, negative behaviors may result. "Know thyself," we are urged.

Danny resented Charles for all the education Charles had, his happy family, and the fact Charles inherited one-half of the family farm. This negative emotion caused Danny to withhold information from Charles about the status of the will's probate and the estate. The irrational thinking on Danny's part was he believed he deserved all his father Donald worked for, thinking carelessly and selfishly the estate was only meant for him and no one else.

Irrational thinking has no moral, ethical or legal basis.

When Charles sent a formal letter to Danny requesting a status report on Mary's estate probate, Danny played a "dirty trick" by showing up unexpectedly and unannounced to Charles's home, perhaps seeking a negotiating advantage through surprise. This brings up the topic of negotiations and meetings.

Meetings, including those in estate planning and execution, as well as probate, should always have an agenda, one communicated to all parties that could be affected by the meeting. That way, no person is caught off-guard, not given adequate time to prepare.

Although subtly, mixed with signs of goodwill, and

sometimes secretly, Danny pursued his mother, manipulating her to secure the executor's role. On the contrary, Mary thought Danny's intentions were noble, not realizing he was manipulating her and hiding multiple issues from her.

For example, Danny hid from his mother and nearby property owners his true intentions concerning an adjacent one acre property which lay between the right-of-way and the mountain farm. Instead, Danny hired an attorney in Jefferson to draw up a quick claim deed and pander the neighbors and community leaders he would donate $2000 to the church. "He also threatened to sue us if we did not cooperate", one of the neighbors told Abigail. In the end he got the deed and donated $350 which infuriated the church leader leading him to agree Danny was a snake in the grass. After Mary prodded Danny, he confessed to her the one-acre plot was "unclaimed." Danny also had the deed changed to his name and hers, but it was all done in secret, as Mary discovered with a separate conversation with the attorney.

Despite Danny's manipulation and controlling, she had a deep abiding love for all her children. She also thought Danny's emotional tactics would change so that the family could be close again.

Mary once told Abigail, "I am thinking about changing the executor because of how Danny is treating me."

Perpetrators like Danny exploit the elderly's vulnerability in a number of ways, most prominently by the use of financial powers of attorney. These documents give the control freaks complete legal authority to do everything, financially, that the elder victim could do: including access bank accounts, or transfer title to a home. Placed into the wrong hands, such as an unethical lawyer's, these powers of attorney become licenses to steal.

Thus, Danny picked and chose, using his personal schedule, what he liked and disliked. Compare this to the *Bible's* admonition to love thy enemies, pray for your enemies, and the ethical Golden Rule, "treat others as you would want to be treated."

Mary did not realize Danny operated by mixing both "good deeds" with unethical business principles, such as bartering and paybacks. He also had a history of hiding information from his ex-wife and family. People hide information in an effort to obtain a competitive advantage, but in family matters this would often be considered a dirty trick.

The attorney selected to represent the estate was not an estate lawyer. Mary and Danny were clients of Jim and Jacky for a long time. The mask that Jim wore as a so called community leader and philanthropic agent was blinding the truth about his loose law practice and Mary's health made her vulnerable to these three power hungry men. The attorney to lead the estate was Jim.

Another local retired attorney David who Charles met on a work project cautioned the co-trustee without slander: "Jim is a political beast, not a legal counselor. Be careful who you put in charge of the money." He was not a man "above reproach," but controversial around the local community and one not considered a particularly moral, ethical man. The ailing mother failed to accept the truth about these two men. Power corrupts even so-called "good men."

Mary still loved all her children, but she was worried most about Danny. She chose to be hopeful that Danny's behavior would change, that he would treat everyone fairly and be transparent. She hoped that his behavior that troubled her would improve if he were put into the role of authority (as the executor). Charles would eventually learn to accept the adage that power tends to corrupt even good men.

Danny and his attorney Jacky were drinking buddies, 'good old boys' who paid each other off, 'under the table', to meet their personal wishes and fuel their greed and power. Jacky did not charge Mary for writing up her will, so that Danny could request from a payback later.

"I'll scratch your back, if you scratch mine," is the mantra of the power-hungry.

Compare using Jacky to an unbiased knowledgeble attorney who did not know the family and was trained in estate law and practices ethical behavior.

Personal bias in estate and family planning causes much contention, either through conscious unfair dealing or through innocent partisanship.

Mary's executor decision was biased by manipulation by the eldest son Danny, which had a major impact on the efficient administration of the estate and ethical practices of both the attorney and the brother-executor.

When big money is involved in an estate even apparent decent folks can corrupt the project resulting in significant negative economic and moral impacts to society.Research demonstrates that most estate planning clients place a higher value on the preservation of family harmony than on the exact amounts of worldly possessions passed on to family members following death.

Unfortunately, Danny's management of both Mary's and Asher's estates has resulted in no harmony, no formal transparent communication, rather a demonstration of greed and control of people. Danny likes to "cut corners" which is considered unethical in business matters.

After two years of the law firm's principal Jim mishandling the estate, Charles is still co-trustee of Asher's multi-million-dollar bank account. Sadly, Jim has yet to met face-to-face to explain the troubling ethical issues surrounding his management practices.

Because of Danny's negative emotions toward Charles and his victim mentality, not being transparent, including failing to appear at the attorney meeting to discuss very important legal matters that would affect the multi-million-dollar estate's beneficiaries, he exhibits cowardice behavior and unethical business practices.

The lesson here: be wise and cautious in choosing a qualified executor. Choosing a family member seems convenient, but it could lead to family division. A better choice would be an unbiased estate attorney.

Wills need not be complicated. Abigail commented that in her work with many people, her clients told her they did not realize that a simple will can be created from online web sites.

I close the book with "If," a poem written by Rudyard Kipling (1865–1936).

Kipling's four eight-line stanzas of advice to his son, written in 1909, have inspired many for a century. Although it is our behavior, not words, that often proves our love, this prose may let my own son know that I have never given up on him. Pride boils within me for his accomplishments, but I know life does not happen without pain; furthermore, many will doubt you.

Donald's dream for his family did not die with his children's breaking the moral code. His legacy lies in Abigail and Charles who despite a tragedy, leaned not on their own understanding but in the counsel of Godly men and women and the wisdom found in the Bible on how to treat people no matter what the cost.

Charles's son still says, "I love you." For that, Charles is forever grateful to know and carry on his dream.

Dream and be an admirable man or woman. Godspeed, my son and daughters.

Here is Kipling's classic poem, "If":

> If you can keep your head when all about you
>   Are losing theirs and blaming it on you;
> If you can trust yourself when all men doubt you,
>   But make allowance for their doubting too;
> If you can wait and not be tired by waiting,
>   Or, being lied about, don't deal in lies,
> Or, being hated, don't give way to hating,
>   And yet don't look too good, nor talk too wise;
>
> If you can dream and not make dreams your master;
>   If you can think and not make thoughts your aim;
> If you can meet with triumph and disaster
>   And treat those two impostors just the same;
> If you can bear to hear the truth you've spoken
>   Twisted by knaves to make a trap for fools,

Or watch the things you gave your life to broken,
    And stoop and build 'em up with worn-out tools;

If you can make one heap of all your winnings
    And risk it on one turn of pitch-and-toss,
And lose, and start again at your beginnings
    And never breathe a word about your loss;
If you can force your heart and nerve and sinew
    To serve your turn long after they are gone,
And so hold on when there is nothing in you
    Except the Will which says to them: "Hold on";

If you can talk with crowds and keep your virtue,
    Or walk with kings nor lose the common touch;
If neither foes nor loving friends can hurt you;
    If all men count with you, but none too much;
If you can fill the unforgiving minute
    With sixty seconds' worth of distance run—
Yours is the Earth and everything that's in it,
    And—which is more—you'll be a Man, my son!

It would not surprise me that, if Kipling were alive today, he would change his last line to something that included daughters, too, though it might be harder to rhyme. Class has no gender.

Shattered Dreams can be used for good, not evil. The Almighty desires for us to have an intimate relationship with Him and to keep an eternal perspective. These two things are the "antidote" to shattered dreams and the key to broken relationships and pain being turned around for good.

Your shattered dreams can come true. Just ask The Almighty.

Godspeed, all.

CPSIA information can be obtained
at www.ICGtesting.com
Printed in the USA
FSHW021213110519
58059FS

9 781478 796336